THE BOOK FOR WORKING WOMEN

(is there any other kind?)

By
The Promethium Chapter of Iota Sigma Pi,
National Honor Society for Women in
Chemistry

Coordinator, J. P. Kilbourn

Aha Publishing, 13275 S. W. Hazel, Beaverton, OR 97005

Copies of this book may be ordered for $30 plus $2.50 postage and handling from Aha Publishing, 13275 S. W. Hazel, Beaverton, OR 97005; $25 of which will be a tax-deductible contribution to the scholarship fund of Promethium Chapter of Iota Sigma Pi.

First Printing 1991
ISBN 0-9628394-1-8
Library of Congress Catalogue Card Number 91-070331

THANKS

A big thank you to those Promethium Chapter Iota Sigma Pi (National Honor Society for Women In Chemistry) members and friends who wrote chapters and contributed anecdotes, or who contributed articles, cartoons, and illustrations. Please see the List of Contributors.

This book would not have been published if it weren't for the favorable response to the previous book "Cartoon-Humor Book for Working Women, Is there any other kind?" I would like to thank those who purchased the copies and wrote with suggestions for improving it.

I would like to thank the Iris M. and Jesse W. Payne Estate for funds to publish the previous book "Cartoon-Humor Book for Working Women, Is there any other kind?"

I would also like to thank my husband, Lee (who also is involved with the Construction Specifications Institute), for typing, editing, and for his support and understanding.

J. P. "Perky" Kilbourn, Ph.D.

PREFACE

We originally wanted to write the book for women scientists. But a publisher encouraged us to broaden the audience because "there aren't enough women scientists."

Yes, there aren't enough women scientists. And there aren't enough women professors, architects, managers, engineers, entrepreneurs, and so on.

The women's movement of the past 20 years has encouraged women to blaze new trails in many traditionally male fields; but, in many cases, the women in those fields are still trail blazers.

We wrote this book for the trail blazers; we wrote this book for all women. Welcome, women, to the business, academic and professional worlds. We know what you are going through and we want you to know that you are not alone.

We have tried to give you a new perspective on your daily struggles for equality and justice. Our perspective will leave you laughing. Our perspective will arm your wit.

Yes, you have a choice about your reaction to the reactionaries who wish you had no ambitions.

This book was conceived at the April, 1988 meeting of the Promethium Chapter of Iota Sigma Pi, national society for women in chemistry. This book was birthed by women from many professions. May you learn from our trials and flumblings. May you blaze your own trail.

Mary Ryan-Hotchkiss, Ph.D.and Jacqueline Fortunata, Ph.D.

LIST OF CONTRIBUTORS

Darlene Angel, (Montes de Oca),
   Customer Service Representative
   Bank of America FSB

James Angel, (Montes de Oca), Darlene's
   brother

The Rev. Annette Arnold-Boyd
   Former Associate Priest, St.
   Stephen's Episcopal Parish
   Present Associate Priest, St. Luke's
   Episcopal Parish

Gary Barclay, Sympathetic husband and
   Illustrator

Jan Barton, Ph.D., Associate Professor
   of Chemistry
   Chemistry Department, Washburn
   University of Topeka

Leona Bayer, M.D., 80+ Years Young

Marie Berg, Ph.D., Retired
   1970 National President, Sigma
   Delta Pi, the Graduate Women in
   Science
   1963-1972 Coordinator of Regional
   Directors
   Iota Sigma Pi, the National Honor
   Society for Women in Chemistry

Judy Blum-Anderson, Ph.D. Candidate
   Education Department, Washington
   State University

Rita Colwell, Ph.D., Director, Maryland
   Biotechnology Institute
   and Professor of Microbiology,
   University of Maryland
   1984-85 National President,
   American Society for Microbiology

Lidia Crosa, Ph.D., Research Associate
   Microbiology Department, Oregon
   Health Sciences University

Dorothy Deline, Assistant to Graduate
   Director
   Marylhurst College

Mildred Dresselhaus, Ph.D.
   Institute Professor of Electrical
   Engineering and Physics
   Massachusetts Institute of
   Technology

Sharon Dunwoody, Professor
   School of Journalism and Mass
   Communication
   University of Wisconsin-Madison

Angela Eggleston, C.P.A.
   Series of articles in Pm Chapter and
   MAL Newsletters of Iota Sigma Pi

Marjorie Enneking, Ph.D., Professor of
   Mathematics
   Portland State University

Jesse Ford, Ph.D., Senior Scientist U.S.
   Environmental Protection Agency
   Corvallis Environmental Research
   Laboratory

Jacqueline Fortunata, Ph.D., Aha
   Publishing

Joseph A. Gascoigne, Executive Director
   Construction Specifications Institute

Carole Gatz, Ph.D., Professor of
   Chemistry
   Portland State University

Shoba Gulati, Ph.D., Associate
   Professor of Mathematics
   St. John's University/College of St.
   Benedict

Diana Hamilton, Certified Construction
   Specifier (CCS)
   Member of Construction
   Specifications I nstitute

Elaine M. Henshon, Director The Dual
   Degree Programs in Liberal Arts
   and Engineering at Smith College

Nicole Hollander, Cartoonist

Ann C. Howe, Ph.D., Professor and
Department Head
Department of Mathematics and
Science Education
College of Education and
Psychology, North Carolina State
University

Alice S. Huang, Ph.D., Professor of
Microbiology and Molecular
Genetics
Department of Pediatrics, Harvard
Medical School
1988-1989 National President
American Society for Microbiology

Elizabeth Ivey, Provost, Macalester
College

J. P. Kilbourn, Ph.D., Laboratory
Director and Owner
Consulting Clinical and
Microbiological Laboratory, Inc.

Sue Kohlhepp, Ph.D., Research
Associate
Gilbert Research Laboratory,
Providence Medical Center

Edna Kunkel, Member of AWIS
Art Editor for AWIS Newsletter

Margie Largent, Architect and
Specification Writer
Past President, 1976, 1986,
Portland Chapter, Construction
Specifications Institute (CSI)

Virginia Lindley, Artist

Nan Lindsley-Griffin, Ph.D., Department
of Geology
University of Nebraska

Marsha Lakes Matyas, Ph.D., Project
Director, Women in Science
American Association for the
Advancement of Science

Melissa Melan, Ph.D., Worcester
Foundation for Experimental
Biology

Leia Melead, N.D., Naturopathic
Physician

Anita Menger, Ph.D., Detmold, Germany

Joann Morey, (Registered) Physician's
Assistant - Certified, (R) PA-C

Carol Mount, B.S., M.S.
An article from Pm Chapter and
MAL Newsletters of Iota Sigma Pi

Amy Mulnix, Ph.D. Candidate,
Entomology Department
Purdue University

Kitty Myers, Certified Construction
Specifier (CCS),
Member of Construction
Specifications Institute (CSI)
Architect and Senior Specifications
Writer, ZGF Partnership

Ellen Quade, Illustrator

Frances Reed, Writer

Linda M. Reilly, Ph.D., Department of
Microbiology
School of Medicine, Vanderbilt
University

B. Jean Richardson, Writer

Abigail Romick, Owner, A.B. Prints,
Inc.

Mary Ryan-Hotchkiss, Ph.D., Analytical
Chemist and Marketing Manager
Textronix, Inc.

Ken Searl, Fellow of the Construction
Specifications Institute (FCSI),
Certified Construction Specifier,
Specifications Writer WEGroup,
Architects

Juliet Popper Shaffer, Ph.D., Department
of Statistics
University of California - Berkeley

Kate Sheehan, Ph.D., Assistant
Professor of Mathematics
Marymount University

Alice Shelly, Fellow of the Construction
Specifications Institute (FCSI),
Certified Construction Specifier
(CCS)
Specifications Writer in Private
Practice

Stephanie Shipp, Editor, Caucus for
Women in Statistics Newsletter

Carol Simmons, Ph.D., Iota Sigma Pi
Member

Elaine Spencer, Ph.D., Retired Associate
Professor of Chemistry
Portland State University

Hazel Stone, Ph.D., (Deceased) Member
of Iota Sigma Pi

Jeanne Sullivan, Assistant Teacher of
Theater Arts
Cairo American College, Cairo,
Egypt

Martha Thompson, Ph.D. Associate
Professor, Dental School, Oregon
Health Sciences University

Inga Vrla, 1988-1989 Past President
Portland Chapter Construction
Specifications Institute (CSI)
Sales Representative National
Marketing

Nancy B. Walters, Program Associate
Minnesota Higher Education
Coordinating Board

Doris C. Warren, Ph.D., Professor of
Chemistry
Houston Baptist University
1981-1984 National President
Iota Sigma Pi, the National Honor
Society for Women in Chemistry

Mary Warren, Children's Books Author

Mary Frances Zimmerman, M.T. (ASCP)
Chemistry Department, Clinical
Pathology Laboratory
Providence Medical Center

Mary Zoll, Ph.D., Technical Writer,
Mary Zoll, Inc.

TABLE OF CONTENTS

Thanks

Preface

List of Contributors

1. . . . . . Stereotypes 1
        Mary Frances Zimmerman

2. . . . . . Role Reversal 11
        Elaine Spencer

3. . . . . . Models and Mentors 26
        Kitty Myers

4. . . . . . Language 37
        Carole Gatz

5. . . . . . Political Satire 46
        Sue Kohlhepp

6. . . . . . Entertaining 49
        J. P. Kilbourn

7. . . . . . Childcare 56
          Sue Kohlhepp

8. . . . . . Coping with Teenagers 62
          J. P. Kilbourn

9. . . . . . How You Look 65
          Mary Ryan-Hotchkiss

10. . . . . Put Downs 73
          Sue Kohlhepp

11. . . . . Your Own Business 84
          Angela W. Eggleston

12. . . . . Hitting Glass Ceiling 96
          Carol Mount.

13. . . . . Hole in Glass Ceiling 100
          J. P. Kilbourn

14. . . . . Women in Academia 105
          Lidia Crosa

1 Stereotypes

Mary Frances Zimmerman

Stereotyping is defined as casting people or things into fixed molds by sex, race, religion or any other characteristic or function. Both culture and media reinforce these stereotyped beliefs.

Male stereotypes are different from female stereotypes in all cultures. Men are assigned the roles of breadwinner, father, power broker, athlete. Women are assigned the roles of mother, nurturer, homemaker, caretaker. These stereotypes, as well as the responsibilities women willingly assume, can be a handicap.

She does affect my backhand.

© 1991 Virginia Lindley, suggested by Carole Gatz

Men and women are stereotyped by our society and culture. For example, men aren't supposed to cry and women are. Men are supposed to be strong and women are supposed to be weak.

Stereotyping in our culture and society is reinforced by words for female/male roles: For example, governor and governess were once equal terms. Now, one is the Governor of a State whether female or male. A governess is one who cares for children. Of course, the position of governess is inferior to that of a Governor.

Some words that once were terms of endearment are now derogatory: hussy, tart, tootsie, and doll.

WHENEVER WE ARGUE REX GETS INTO THE SUBMISSION POSE.

If one doesn't follow the stereotypes of one's culture, one is labeled as different. Thankfully, cultural stereotypes are changing!

The term "tomboy" once identified girls who participated in sports or went into professions dominated by men. Since women now play most sports and enter all professions, the term is rarely used. Women no longer have to be worried about being tomboys or liking math.

The term "sissy" is the male counterpart to the female term tomboy. A sissy is a boy who is effeminate. Since society is beginning to accept men who are less macho, including homosexual, sissy is rarely used. Men are learning nurturing skills and are entering service jobs such as nursing and teaching that were once restricted to women.

© 1991 Virginia Lindley, suggested by J. P. Kilbourn

Note that women are not just doing men's jobs by acting like men in the industrial/business workplace. Women are bringing their caring/nurturing traditions to the industrial/business workplace.

> # Herman Miller's Secrets of Corporate Creativity
> ## BUSINESS WORLD by George Melloan
>
> . . . Mr. DePree, (Chairman and CEO of Herman Miller, Inc.) also expects a "tremendous social change" in all workplaces. "When I first started working 40 years ago, a factory supervisor was focused on the product. Today it is drastically different, because of the social milieu. It isn't unusual for a worker to arrive on his shift and have some family problem that he doesn't know how to resolve. The example I like to use is a guy who comes and says 'this isn't going to be a good day for me, my son is in jail on a drunk-driving charge and I don't know how to raise bail.' What that means is that if the supervisor wants productivity he has to know how to raise bail. . . "
>

Similarly, men are bringing their management/business skills to women-dominated service industries. As a result of men entering these industries, service workers are now better paid. Or, perhaps men are now entering these service industries because the workers are better paid.

Society must accept the qualities of both sexes in either sex.

There is a new stereotype: that of a Superwoman. A Superwoman is a woman who can make a home, rear a family, please a husband and have a successful career, neglecting none of the above. This is not an ideal model for today's woman; she is being replaced by one in which she and her partner share goals and the efforts required to reach them.

> Women don't need flexible hours or child care or more maternity leave. What they need are WIVES.

Mildred Dresselhaus comments on her experiences as a woman in a man's field:

My career in science and technology has been interesting and exciting beyond all expectation. And it has been filled with unusual and unexpected events, some of which would not have happened, had I not been a woman. Women in my age group who have made careers in science and technology are few and far between. For that reason we are highly visible and have had opportunities and responsibilities that are unique. In many cases, we are the first women to have been chosen for some particular assignment, and with this opportunity lies a responsibility to perform well, so that a similar opportunity will soon be extended to another woman. As a professor in a field where there are few women, I have also felt a responsibility to perform effectively on the job, to serve as a role model for women students and younger faculty, as well as for my male colleagues.

Over the years, I have experienced a number of amusing or unusual incidents in the pursuit of my career, and I have chosen three for your anthology. The first relates to my student days at Hunter College, which at that time was a women's college with a good academic reputation and a large number of women faculty members in their Math and Science Departments. Though the number of students in the physical sciences was small, we were led to believe that women could succeed in any area of academic studies. This was further confirmed when the GI's arrived home after being discharged from the Armed Services and wanted to complete their college educations.

After World War II many of the women's colleges, such as Hunter College, opened their doors to the returning GI's. Since the most talented of the GI's did not come to Hunter College, the women students competed very successfully against the men in math and science classes. Thus it wasn't until well into my college days that I discovered that women were not supposed to be able to learn math and science. My introduction to these prejudices came when my thesis advisor told me that graduate fellowship support for women students was a waste of money because women would not make much use of their technical training. The facts proved otherwise, and the four women students who overlapped with me at the University of Chicago all went on to highly productive careers in physics. Even the professor changed his position on the efficacy of educating women graduate students within ten years of my completion of the Ph.D. Degree.

I don't train women in science because they do not make use of their technical training.

© 1991 Virginia Lindley, suggested by Mildred Dresselhaus

Later, when I was a Postdoc at Cornell, there arose a need to find somebody to teach a junior level course in electromagnetism, because the professor who had been given that assignment left the University quite unexpectedly at the start of the semester. At that late stage, it was difficult to find a substitute, since everyone on the physics faculty was already overcommitted. And so it was that I volunteered for the assignment.

After much discussion by the physics faculty, I was allowed to take over the all-male class. The main concern was that I wouldn't be able to win the respect of the students and get them to do the homework. I took this on as a challenge and worked very hard to give the students interesting and challenging homework assignments. In fact, I have remembered this concern for many years and have been especially diligent in the preparation of homework assignments. Rewards that have come to me from these early teaching efforts were attracting some gifted students to research careers in physics. Moreover, the teaching experience acquired from these volunteer assignments directly led to my appointment as a full professor at MIT a decade later.

Many years later, when I was the Laboratory Director of MIT's Center for Materials Science and Engineering, one of my duties was to show visitors around the laboratory. For the most part this worked out very well, because the visitors would normally make contact well in advance of their arrival, and my secretary would welcome them when they arrived in the outer office and call me to come out of the inner office to greet them.

But, one fine Saturday when there was no secretary, a Japanese delegation arrived to be shown around the laboratory. Since Saturday morning is often a workday in a Japanese University, they expected to find someone in the office to show them around. There was nothing scheduled for me on that day, and I therefore decided to do a cleanup job in the lab and came in appropriately attired. It was in this state that I encountered the Japanese delegation in the hallway.

They asked to be shown to the Director's office. I then offered to take them there and they were pleased. I soon took their coats and hung them up and asked them what they wanted to see. They all chimed in, almost in unison that they came to see the Director. I then tried to explain to them that I was the Director, but to no avail. They looked so forlorn. Alas, my appearance fell so far short of their expectation of an MIT Laboratory Director!

I took them all into my inner office, gave them all annual research reports, and tried to give them a presentation about research in the Laboratory. I doubt that they heard a word of what I said, because they had such a hard time believing that I could direct such a large research laboratory. It is hard to say what was the long term effect of this encounter on the Japanese visitors, but for me it was a feeling that I always must be prepared for the unexpected when I arrive at the Laboratory. A woman in science is a public figure and must behave accordingly. The customer is always right and should not be disappointed.

Rita Colwell writes: The struggle of women scientists to be recognized and, more importantly, to be appointed to the highest rank of top management positions, is definitely not over. The struggle continues. It has been elevated from a battle to get women appointed to tenure track positions rather than "associates" or "super graduate student/research associate" (as was the case twenty years ago), to the more difficult struggle to have women appointed to positions of deans, vice presidents, and presidents of universities, industries, foundations, etc. It seems that women scientists now are conceded to be equally qualified to carry out research and to win prizes for research, but they bump up against "the glass ceiling" when it is time to be promoted to full professor, department head, or president. That needs to be recognized and not glossed over by the fact that many women have been appointed to tenure track positions as assistant professors and, with superb track records, to tenured associate professors.

When I was to graduate from Purdue University in 1956, I had been accepted to medical school but was going to be married just before graduation and decided to stay on at Purdue to obtain a Master's Degree so that my husband, who was then a graduate student in Chemistry, could complete a Master's so that we could both go on to another Institution for our Ph.D.'s. The decision was mine since I wanted to do my Ph.D. at another institution so that I would have broader experience. Upon approaching the Chairman for a fellowship, I was told, "Fellowships are not wasted on women."

About twenty years later, I was an officer of the International Union of Microbiological Societies and was attending the International Congress of the Union in Tokyo. Stepping out of the elevator in the Headquarters Hotel, I bumped into this former Department Chairman. He was most friendly and he graciously and enthusiastically introduced me to his colleagues as "one of his prize undergraduate students when he was at Purdue!" I remembered the statement he made twenty years earlier, which very nearly derailed me from graduate school. I thanked him for "not wasting a fellowship on me" since it gave me an excellent opportunity, to learn genetics. Learning genetics was far more valuable in my career than continuing for another year in the bacteriology department would have been!

According to statistics you don't waste them on minority races either.

EXCUSES FOR NOT HIRING WOMEN:

"You will leave and get married." But you are already married.

"You will leave to have children." But you already have children.

"You should be home with your children." The children are in college.

"Your husband has a job." Your husband died, you are divorced, he is unemployed, or he doesn't make enough money.

"You are too old and will quit work as soon as trained." Your own or your husband's pension is too small.

Contributed by J. P. Kilbourn

"A woman is not given a job because she is overqualified." If she reapplies and leaves out her advanced degrees she is told she is underqualified.

Contributed by Leia Melead

Representative-at-Large Report; Juliet Shaffer

It is easy to focus on the weak area in women and the strong areas in men, thus justifying decisions against women applicants.

I remember especially two situations in which I felt this process was operating. A woman applicant, with superb credentials, the only woman among the finalists, was eliminated on the grounds that the Department already had enough faculty in her specialized area (although the ad had stated that the Department was looking for qualified candidates regardless of area). The next year a man was hired in the same area. When I asked about the discrepancy, I was told that although the area wasn't a high priority, he was very good.

A woman applicant was denied tenure on the grounds that she hadn't done enough research and that an adequate level of research was essential for tenure. A short time later a man, in spite of a weak research record, was given tenure because he had important clinical skills.

2 Role Reversal

Elaine Spencer

"Role Reversal" has meaning only when the sexes are stereotyped. The sexes are stereotyped in our society.

© 1991 Gary Barclay

Since this country was established, the man has worn pants, even though in the early days they might have been satin and tied with ribbons at the knees for dress occasions.

Current gender traditions in the United States, surprisingly, are not really very old. The man of the family has always been an important provider but only in the last century have men left home daily in large numbers to work. Before, the United States was mostly agricultural and men were farmers who worked their own land. With the industrial revolution, men left home for the factory or office.

1800's

© 1991 Gary Barclay

EARLY 1900's

© 1991 Gary Barclay

LATE 1900's

© 1991 Gary Barclay

When a husband, out of a sense of fairness, does his part to help out at home, he becomes the object of jokes.

His incompetence in household tasks is the butt of countless jokes, cartoons, and TV situation comedies.

These jokes not only reinforce the unwillingness of men to do women's work but also build up the egos of the women whose expertise has been undervalued. Women need to let go of the role of being "Queen of the Kitchen" if they want men to help with household chores.

© 1991 Gary Barclay

Women in business, industry and the professions are stereotyped as emotional, unstable, capricious and incapable. Women may not be portrayed as strong, capable, wise and respected mentors, but they are also not represented as paternalistic and tyrannical as male bosses often are. Women have successfully managed their families and homes for centuries. Now they are becoming successful managers in the business world. This is true not only in the United States but also in other countries. The following cartoon was sent by Anita Menger, from Detmold Germany:

... und zu guter Letzt

„Wenn mich nicht alles täuscht, ist unser neuer Chef eine Frau!"

As far as I can see –
our new boss is a woman!

(translated by Anita Menger)

The stereotype lingers that women are secretaries and housewives, and if they stay within a stereotyped role, they must manage men through clever diplomacy or outright deceit.

These stereotypical women are supposed to manipulate powerful men to their own advantage quite effortlessly and to flatter the men into accepting a woman's good ideas as the man's own, with no need to give credit or reward of any kind to a women.

Perhaps times are changing. Sometimes there is a grudging acknowledgement that a woman is doing a good job. Modern management theory suggests that greater openness and recognition of contributions produces better long-term results.

© 1991 Ellen Quade

Many husbands and fathers are assuming equal roles in the family.

Mother's Secret   on Father's Day
Ellen Goodman
Nevertheless, it turns out that sharing the work of raising children also means sharing the power over children's lives. Sharing the power - even the kind you didn't fully recognize - is harder than expected. Letting go of child power, giving up the central role in a child's life, can be as hard as letting go of purse power. It doesn't sound like a dramatic struggle. But it can come with a sudden, internal wrench.
© 1988 The Boston Globe Newspaper Company

Women are not equal to men; in a crucial way, they are superior. Women hold the power that gives meaning to all human life: the ability to create the next generation. To be accepted as a mate, a man has to show he can provide for a woman's potential children. So he must take risks leading to big rewards.

© 1988 Success

© 1991 Ellen Quade

Men are inspired by marriage. A successful marriage used to be measured by a home in a nice neighborhood, good education for the children and expensive clothes. To obtain these things a man needed to be an action-oriented provider-aggressive, a team player, a leader, optimistic, brave and smart.

The American economy now favors women in the executive suite. No longer an action-oriented industrial society that creates merchandise, this nation needs sensitive leaders who work well in service-oriented companies. Women know how to communicate, use their intuition and reach consensus, which are skills required by these new enterprises. The Industrial Age is giving way to the Information Age. Women's skills will be needed in the new work environment.

Books such as *Games Mother Never Taught You: Corporate Gamesmanship for Women* (Harrigan, 1977) are teaching women how to cope in the business world and new ways to do business. Books such as *In a Different Voice* (Gilligan, 1982) can teach men that the world is a gift not to be destroyed. Women don't like to play games where people win and lose, get their feelings hurt and feel bad.

Women see war in terms of waste, death and what it means to raise a child. Men should rethink the male notion of patriotic sacrifice and the notion of the "other" as enemy.

Women have long sacrificed themselves to preserve the lives of their children. Men should learn how to sacrifice themselves to preserve the lives of their children not the life style of their children. They can start by cutting the defense budget, not the health and education budget.

In conclusion, a reversal of roles or at least a blurring of roles benefits all people. Men could become more like women and develop their nurturing skills. At the same time, women could become more like men and develop their assertiveness skills.

3 Models and Mentors

Kitty Myers

The traditional way to get ahead is through the "Good Old Boys" network. You follow a successful role model or, better yet, an experienced good old boy offers to show you the ropes and introduces you to the right people. To their loss, women professionals are excluded from the old boys network by the overt and covert actions of male colleagues.

The bad news is that women often exclude themselves. As little girls, women form friendships based on closeness and intimacy, not on attaining a common goal. Thus, they find it hard to form the kind of relationships necessary for professional success. The good news is that women can choose other kinds of relationships--either to learn the male way of relating or to develop new ways of their own.

Unfortunately, female role models and mentors are scarce. This means we must help. Often, women compete with each other, rather than help each other.

Competition among men is respected and admired. It does not hurt a cooperative relationship among equals. Men often form a relationship to achieve a common end without concern for personal feelings. It is becoming more common for women to do so also.

Stereotypes interfere with the availability of role models and mentors for women, increasing women's isolation and lack of opportunity in the workplace.

Women must form their own "good old girls" networks.

There are good role models in the world outside of work. There are many roles to consider: wife, mother, volunteer, friend, lover, etc. Sometimes a mother, aunt, grandmother, or older friend serves as a role model, but often we learn to nurture in ways that hurt ourselves. We sometimes learn from our spouses or lovers how to be more selfish or we repeat self-destructive patterns.

Redefining our roles and keeping a healthy balance is a new challenge for most women. The positive rewards of the workplace encourage people to spend more time there.

Power, recognition for a job well done and money make a stay-at-home life look dull. An interesting and challenging job, a caring family, and careful balancing can make a life as rich as a tapestry, in which all the threads come together in a beautiful design.

Nancy B. Walters is discovering that women and minorities may be failing not so much from lack of ability as from ignorance of the steps needed to succeed. In one experimental learning program for women and minority college students the students work collaboratively in small groups. The workshop approach encourages students to critique each other's work, students discover there is more than one "right" way to solve a problem. The students learn to share information in a non-competitive way so they all can win. The workshops also teach the students a pattern for networking and mentoring they can use in their careers.

Doris Warren writes: As we reach the point in our careers where we serve as mentors, let us serve wisely. As a parent teaches independence and then must let go, let us serve as mentors and then applaud the independent steps forward of the women we are mentoring. They must then make their own choices. Even if these are not the choices we might make - let them go free and make their own mistakes and be responsible for their own triumphs.

Doris advises that as a mentor, may she never feel threatened, but instead always sit back and be happy for the successes, help heal the hurt and allow the women she has mentored to be an equal and a friend.

Alice S. Huang writes: In my travels over the past several years, I have met a large number of women professionals, particularly in the biological sciences. Many have impressive credentials. Although unsaid at these meetings, I sensed a common ground among all of us, whether we are from the East or the West, whether we work in academia or elsewhere, whether we are novices or old hands, and whether we have been privileged or poor. Every single woman has seen or experienced some form of gender bias. This can come from individuals with the best of intentions.

What we have in common is a quiet determination to use whatever power we may have to support one another and to encourage change away from gender bias. This I know by their actions; they remain consistent. Therefore, no matter how old, how masculine and how cold a woman might appear, remember she knows and she will help if you ask.

© 1991 Kitty Myers

Janice Barton writes about subtle discrimination in the October, 1988 Iota Sigma Pi Member at Large Newsletter: A series of articles in the Kansas State newspaper concerned subtle discrimination in our schools and universities. The articles caused me to think about an experience I had this summer while attending a meeting on the role of undergraduate research in the education process. A woman scientist from NIH was one of several speakers at this conference; she was a good speaker but not the best of the day or the conference. As soon as she finished, a middle aged male colleague sitting behind me exclaimed about her being articulate. I told him that was a sexist statement. He was surprised by my comment until I pointed out that she is a well-educated spokesperson for a national funding agency, and that he would not and did not make similar comments about the male speakers.

One of the most difficult barriers to full equality is the early nurturing and education that shape our views and our expectations of the roles and capabilities of the sexes. Legal barriers may be falling but we will be struggling with attitudes for some time to come. Many men and women are not aware that common things that are said and done are not only discriminatory, but tend to perpetuate myths and discrimination. We need to help sensitize our acquaintances to these subtle forms of discrimination.

© 1991 Kitty Myers

Ann C. Howe also writes: Subtle and overt discrimination have been so much a part of my life and have caused me so much unhappiness that I cannot yet laugh about it. I could bore you terminally by recounting the personal and professional challenges that I would not have encountered if I had been a man.

I started in chemistry but eventually found my way into science education. One would think that science education would be more hospitable to women than 'pure' science but it is, actually, only a tiny bit more accepting and open than other fields. However, at every point in my career someone, usually a woman but sometimes a man, has reached out to support and encourage me. A woman

Page 32

persuaded me to go back to school to start a new career, a journal editor heard the first paper I ever gave at a professional meeting and offered to publish it, another person persuaded a dean that I was the best qualified candidate for my first real academic appointment.

Now that I am something of an "elder statesperson" in my field I do not forget to reach out to encourage others, especially young women, whenever I see an opportunity. It is the least I can do - and maybe the most important thing I can do.

Mary Ryan-Hotchkiss writes as follows: I would not be involved in Iota Sigma Pi if it were not important to maintain contacts with women scientists. I would agree that when I was in graduate school these contacts were not as important. The graduate school society was a small one and I felt a great deal of camaraderie with professors and the other graduate students. There were always times to get together to socialize or talk about ideas. I received a great deal of support in pursuing my objectives. I also enjoyed Iota Sigma Pi then but noticed that the active people tended to be the older students like myself, those with families or at least husbands. We had additional complications in our lives that many of the other graduate students weren't aware of. It was helpful to see other people with similar problems persist and succeed in their studies.

Now I am working, again in a predominantly male environment. I find Iota Sigma Pi enjoyable and helpful because it again provides me with role models, helps me to meet people with similar interests and problems and introduces me to a broader range of professional (not necessarily female) contacts than my other professional societies provide. I also feel a responsibility to be a role model to our student members.

Statistics from the Harvard Business School class of 1975 showed that about half of these 82 women sought senior-level executive positions. About 45 percent desired a more even balance between their personal lives and work. Interestingly, both groups included single and married women, with and without children. The difference seems to be that some women are committed to full time careers and others are not, which is the same for men.

Leona M. Bayer writes as follows: If young women choose a complex lifestyle involving career, marriage and children, it is important that each element of the design be satisfying. I found the choice of medicine as a profession to be a solid base because it offered so much flexibility. Good health is another fundamental requirement, almost a sine qua non. A generous mate with a strong ego, who shares most of one's cherished values, will happily facilitate the mutual enterprise. But even under the best of circumstances, the multifaceted life is sometimes overwhelming. At one moment in my middle years, I wrote this lament:

My day is a strainer that sifts out
a pyramiding pile of never-finished business.

The new morning presents its miscellaneous tasks:
the day's routine, the visitor from Togoland,
the telegram that just precedes another guest descending from the
    distant air.

Firmly I pass the desk stacked high with unread pamphlets,
the press of medicine and world affairs, the photographs to mount,
the letters needing answer, the meeting to arrange.
Maybe this evening?

Yes.   After the festive dinner, after the song and talk,some bills are
    paid, some notes are sent.
Dear Congressman: do work to make the UN strong, to stop the tests;
do keep our civil liberties alive, our wilderness intact.

The pillow brings a drowsy, brief reprise,
like a bright kaleidoscopic pattern on a bolt of modern cloth
the day glides by, another entry on the scroll of overflowing years.

Not bad, but not enough to drain the ever rising residue of jobs
    undone.
Will unknown friends look after what remains?
Perhaps.   Perhaps in India or Iowa or France,
each in her own way.

© Leona M. Bayer

Leona concludes that despite the complications and
frustrations, she looks back from her mid-eighties grateful that

I had it all!

Women who have juggled a career and family can help those
women who want to "have it all." Pass along the tips you learned the
hard way by trial and error.

4 Language

Carole Gatz

"Actions speak louder than words." "Sticks and stones can break my bones but words will never hurt me." Is language important? Yes. Is what people say to each other insignificant compared with what they do to each other? No.

Although sticks and stones are worse than a verbal attack, words can hurt.

Psychiatrists and the legal system both recognize the serious and long-lasting harm that words can do. Slander, verbal abuse, and sexual harassment are all serious forms of verbal attack.

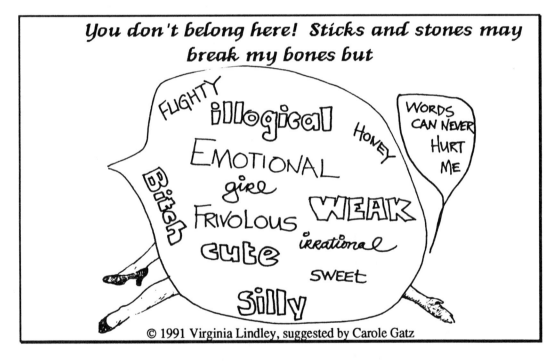

© 1991 Virginia Lindley, suggested by Carole Gatz

Even careless or thoughtless words can have a negative effect that their speaker may not even realize, much less intend. Blacks have raised the general consciousness to the implicit racism of words such as "boy" and of using first names for some people and "Mr. last name" for others. Feminists immediately recognized the same kinds of verbal thoughtlessness. The first name/last name usage is sexist. When all of the workers are female and all of the bosses are male a line has been drawn.

A joke based on a stereotype patronizes women. It is unacceptable to joke about blacks as being lazy or eating too much watermelon, but it is still ok to joke about women who can't balance their checkbooks or who spend too much on clothing. Unfortunately, stereotypes are ingrained in our society and are often tolerated or even accepted by women. A woman may even encourage these jokes for the attention or to feel a part of the group.

Of course warmth, friendliness, and good humor are always welcome aspects of office conversation. The subject matter, the intellectual level, and the tone should respect the feelings of others.

Language presents challenges. We object to being called "Honey" or "Sweetie," but what about "Madame Chairman"? Is "firefighter" better than "fireman," "mail carrier" better than "mailman"? A help-wanted ad advertised for. a "seamster," the generic word for "seamstress." "Sewer" doesn't have the right sound. We all learned back in grammar school that "man" means "man or woman" and that "he" means "he or she." Although we understand this at the intellectual level, we often misunderstand at the gut level. A job description that begins, "We are looking for a man who . . . " excludes women. They are looking for a man, although they might accept a woman, if one applies. Job discrimination has not been ended by good will or by good sense, or even by law.

A patriarchal society evolved the use of "man" and "he" to include both men and women. Now there are writer's guidelines to keep sexist language out of official documents and the media. We should clean up our language.

BS by KS
Basic Specs by Ken Searl

In the October 1983 issue of *The Construction Specifier* magazine, there is an article on Page 15 entitled "Legal Points" discussing the role of women in federal construction contracts. Two clauses have been included in federal prime contracts which state utilization of women-owned businesses (Concerns over $10,000). Clause (B) states the contractor "agrees to use his best efforts to carry out this policy in the award of sub-contracts to the fullest performance of this contract."

The government is trying to help women-owned businesses (at least 51% owned by a woman or women who also control and operate it).

I guess women can have only sub-contracting firms. Evidently the federal boys do not recognize a contractor could be other than a man hence the word "his" is used in Clause (B).

For many years now I have taken the words "he" and "his" out of our contract documents, and usually when I write a letter I do not begin with a salutation, especially not "Dear Sir." How do I know the person the letter is intended for is a male or a female? Our fearless Editor once received a letter addressed to Margie Largent that began "Dear Sir." Good Grief! Can't this world ever call a spade a spade; why do they have to call it a shovel? I know it's going to be difficult, but we should all try. Once you label something with a name, it is darned hard to change it. For example many people and some that should know better call concrete "cement," so you can see the problem we have in acknowledging that there just could be a woman at the head of an organization and in full control. By now you may be asking just what does all this have to do with specifications Well, as you know when I was asked to write a column titled "Basic Specs by Ken Searl" (BS by KS), I was told I could write what I wanted to do so long as it was fit to print. So there!

© 1991 Virginia Lindley, suggested by Carole Gatz

The following response was received and published:
Dear Ken

I've been reading and enjoying your column in *The Predicator* for many years, but your December article regarding sexism in contract documents and other construction industry publications and correspondence has prompted me to finally write a letter to you.

Seven years ago, after receiving 210 letters from manufacturers (as follow-ups to CSI Convention Booth Registrations) entitled "Dear Sir," "Gentlemen," and "Dear Mr. Shelly," I started my own little campaign for recognition of the fact that there are women in CSI (Construction Specifications Institute).

I wrote a letter to each of the offending manufacturers, explaining the situation, and received a number of positive thoughtful responses. The following year, 14 of these manufacturers had corrected their salutations to non-sexist, but 8 other manufacturers with previous non-sexist salutations had fallen into the "Dear Sir" category. I again wrote all offending manufacturers, only to find the numbers the following years essentially unchanged. After lamenting this situation to Hans "Bill" Meier, he wrote a good article in *The Specifier* on the subject, which I'm sure you remember. I had hopes that Bill's article would bring a dramatic change in the numbers, but, alas, I still received a lot of "Dear Sir" letters.

Evidently the originators of manufacturers' letters change so much from year to year that a personal letter to the originator accomplished little lasting impression. Only continual broad exposure of the problem via widely read publications will bring about change. Thanks for your help via your column.

Short of counting through the CSI Roster (which I'm not about to do!), I have no way of knowing the percentage of women in CSI, but my best guess would be 15%-20% women and increasing every year.

It is a continual puzzle to me why a manufacturer will go to the expense of mailing me a catalog worth $15 to $20, type a personalized cover letter with my name and address, and then start the letter "Dear Sir." This practice immediately creates a negative response to their company by 15% -20% of the letter recipients. Positive responses can be attained by starting "Good Morning,"

"Dear Conventioneer," "Dear Exhibit Visitor," "Dear CSI Member," or numerous other salutations.

A fine example of the increasing importance of women in construction was the review in *The Predicator* of your November meeting where both of the speakers on "Removal of Hazardous Materials" were women in very responsible positions. This is a definite trend in the construction industry: more female students in Architectural and Engineering schools, more women representing products, more women in contracting and subcontracting, and generally a larger number of women in all phases of the construction industry.

I'm not an avid women's libber, but have become increasingly aware of some of the subtle sexist attitudes and unintentional oversights which create male directions where none should occur. There are some titles to which I have no objection, such as "Chairman" and of course "Fellow," which I feel are generic and well understood. But I do resent being called "Sir," "Gentleman," and "Mr."

Well, I've rambled on long enough on the subject and you obviously don't need my sermons. Thanks again for your leadership and support for recognition of women in construction.

Aloha!   Alice

Alice was the first woman to become a Fellow of the Construction Specifications Institute and is a Certified Construction Specifier in Honolulu, Hawaii.

In 1989, three of the five awards for Chapter Newsletters for the Construction Specifications Institute, were given to women editors. CSI has had women Chapter Presidents and Region Directors, and National Vice Presidents but no National President. The time will come.

In 1985 the Margie Largent (mentioned in Ken's BS by KS), was elected President of the Portland Chapter of The Construction Specifications Institute. She writes:

From the President

One of the rewards of being an officer in any CSI Chapter is the *CSI Administrative References*. I suppose all associations have such guides, but I'll bet none surpasses CSI's in quality! It is great;

every officer should read it from cover to cover, and I urge all CSI members to try to borrow one.

As a "how-to" reference book it is amazingly complete. I have possessed and shared many, and know most officers read their job descriptions. But few officers read it in toto.

Since the Tri-Region Conference in Monterey, I have read every page, to my benefit and I hope Its own. It has one language flaw, which doesn't detract from the content, but does keep it from being the quality communication tool that is intended. The earlier portions (almost all) of the book are sexist. The newer portions are less so, so I thought it would eventually evolve into a simpler generic reference -- maybe not in my lifetime!

At "Tri-Region" an Institute (South Region) officer made a particularly offensive (to me) comment about the use of the word CHAIRPERSON . . . "chairman being neither male nor female" . . . and I commented to a (N. W. Region) officer sitting on my left that I could "live" with the word "chairman," but that the President's part of the guide is replete with "he, his, him, etc.." and I felt it was time to throw out these "crutches and canes" and use language that was -- if not "person-able" at least more presentable.

He, Paul Edlund, said, "Margie, why don't you just sit down and edit the whole book -- it won't get done unless someone makes such a presentation -- do it." I've done it, along the lines of the appendices. So, my love affair with the *CSI Administrative References* has grown.

Margie followed through on her column and wrote the Executive Director of the Construction Specifications Institute as follows:

I have been informed, Mr. Gascoigne, that the Institute is about to update the *CSI Administrative References*. My informant, Paul Edlund, knew I had recently edited this *CSI Administrative References* for sexist language and he suggested I mail my "edited" copy to you to possibly be included in the "update." I have not included those pages that I found in good order.

Our chapter has one vocal member who objects to "chair" being used in lieu of "Chairman," but I found that there are many places in the *CSI Administrative References* where "chair" is used and it does not sound or look awkward. Please consider the word "chair" or chair- and a space behind where either man or woman

Page 42

could be inserted as needed. I, too, found "chairperson" a trifle affected or forced and would prefer, personally to be called "chair." Motions have been "tabled" - why not by "chairs"?

The *CSI Administrative References* is a fine publication. Please eliminate the last "shall" and get the "chairs" in order - without he, him, his doing the work. Considering what the Construction Specifications Institute has done with specifications language, I think it can clean up the *CSI Administrative References* without a single "person."

Mr. Gascoigne responded as follows:

Thanks very much for your input on the *CSI Administrative References*. We agree with your comments in general.

Let me give you a little background. For years the *CSI Administrative References* had been on computer tape with an outside agency. During the course of many annual updates the whole nine yards deteriorated to a cut-and-paste operation that became almost impossible and did not address your sexist (sic) objections.

Last year, we took the bull by the horns for a complete rewrite under the able direction of our Katherine Bates, Manager of Public Relations. It just so happens that we are at final review stage before putting it into our own computers. We have hard copy and diskettes. When finally massaged it will go to our typesetter directly from computer input.

I will debate some of your points. Chairman versus Chair, for example. Chairman is correct and conforms to the practice of the National Association of Parliamentarians, whose members are female (note my preferential sequence) and male. While I appreciate your remarks about the Bylaws and Institute Policy, they are cast in concrete, verbatim actions of the membership and the Board. They will not be touched in the upcoming edition. Though your suggestions are administrative in character, those are legal documents and cannot be changed without formal action. I do promise to take them up with Secretary Weldon Nash for consideration in the coming year.

Carol Simmons, Iota Sigma Pi member, writes as follows: I have noticed the following, especially when I'm looking for information concerned with the computer industry. If I write CAROL SIMMONS, the mail comes back as CARL

SIMMONS. If I write C. SIMMONS, the answer is MR. C. SIMMONS. The chemical companies are not this bad!

Carol advised she had an even more annoying time with some telephone solicitors (on another matter) who would ask for Mr. Simmons - as soon as someone at the lab said "There's no Mr. Simmons" or "You mean Miss Simmons" the solicitor would hang up. It took 2 months and 100 calls before they'd listen!

When I sign letters "J. P. Kilbourn," I receive replies that begin "Dear Mr. Kilbourn."

Nan Lindsley-Griffin uses the salutation "Gentlebeings." She finds it especially useful when dealing with administrators, bureaucrats, tax auditors, and other creatures whose terrestrial origin may be in doubt.

Hazel Stone, an eighty plus year old member of Iota Sigma Pi, who died in 1988, wrote this poem in 1983.

UNISEX VOCABULARY

HuMAN's out, and so is perSON,
FeMALE, woMEN, join the list:
All glorify the masculine;
From their use desist.

PEOPLE is the only term
Allowed, collectively:
Logically it follows,
An individual's Pe.

All the problems disappear:
Chairpe, workpe, firepe,
Policepe, even Congresspe!
We name them happily.

Discriminating pronouns,
Those hims and hers and shes,
All are reduced by this device
To briefly spoken pes.

"Pe came peself to see us,"
"Pe's not here tonight,"
"Hang pe's jacket on the hook."
How peculiarly right!

Even rest room captions
We can more quickly see,
When MEN and WOMEN are replaced
By a simple Pe!

5 Political Satire

Sue Kohlhepp

Men have traditionally created cartoons and comic strips. Now there are several cartoonists who are women. When a man, such as Garry Trudeau, protested the political situation in his comic strip "Doonesbury," he became a satirist. When Cathy Guisewite, whose "Cathy" cartoons are usually about baby boomer problems such as dating and child rearing, raised questions and gave statistics on what has been happening to women for the last few years, her comic strips are pulled. Are women not supposed to be political? Are the political views of women unimportant?

For example, in one cartoon (dated 11-3-88), Cathy's friend, Andrea, rattles off statistics to her boy friend on how bad it is for women. Her friend responds that it is annoying to hear statistics that substantiate a person's views. Politics should be discussed with non-partisan and non-subjective facts. Andrea responds, "Four out of the last ten vice presidents became president."

In another cartoon (dated 10-28-88), more statistics are quoted, this time during a conversation between Cathy and Andrea. Andrea states that many people are unaware of the statistics and the effect of the government's policy on the working women. Andrea likens the government to a baby: the government doesn't look dangerous when it is sleeping.

What happens when women cartoonists make statements against an administration or point out that an administration is not responsive to women? Is dating an acceptable topic for a cartoon but the results of dating not? The results of dating may be a single parent family, an abortion, or a maternity leave if the mother must combine career and family.

Another cartoon (dated 11-2-88), emphasizes the plight of women who try to combine career and family. Andrea quotes statistics to her daughter, Zenith. Zenith's responds by stuffing the political fliers down the toilet. Child rearing is an acceptable topic as long as it ignores the absence of adequate, government-supported child care facilities. Statistics on the plight of women in the work force are compiled by the government but apparently can not be used in cartoons.

In another cartoon (dated 10-27-88), Andrea discusses her plight as a working mother with Zenith. The concept of giving power to individual companies to promote fairness in the workplace sounds fine until one realizes that the average company is not fair when it comes to working mothers.

In another cartoon (dated 10-31-88), Andrea dresses Zenith as the Statue of Liberty for Halloween. In exchange for trick or treat candy, Zenith hands out fliers explaining how important it is for each and every person to vote. Andrea tells Cathy the logic behind what Zenith is doing. Zenith's thought bubble contains the statement "Therapy by age 5." Because of the apathy towards national elections, there is a call to return to the smoke-filled rooms to pick candidates. Did we really have better candidates on the ballot when they were picked in a smoke-filled room?

The cartoon (dated 10-24-88), shows Cathy trying to make an informed decision about the candidates. In frustration, Cathy wonders if there is still hope for life on Mars.

"Cathy" Strips re-ignite debate over political content of comics
Beverly Beyette

Is there a double standard that permits political issues in "Doonesbury" but not in "Cathy"?

Not really, said Lee Salem, editorial director for Universal Press Syndicate, which distributes both strips. "Garry, of course, is accepted as a traditional satirist. Cathy, although she often deals directly with women's issues, has certainly not done it before in this overt a manner."

© 1988 LA Times-Washington Post Service

In the cartoon (dated 10-25-88), Cathy's mom talks back to the television set. She responds like a mother to the political rhetoric. Study new techniques for balancing the budget? Quit spending money you don't have. Write a report about our polluted oceans and rivers? If you mess it up, you clean it up. Spend money on defense? Spend money on the homeless. Cathy's mom concludes by suggesting that the country needs a mother. But if women are willing to accept the responsibility for society's woes, shouldn't they have a say in creating such woes?

In the cartoon (dated 11-4-88), Andrea is telling Cathy and her mom about the lies behind the "booming economy":

1. The economy requires most mothers to work outside the home to help pay the bills.

2. Legislation that would help struggling working mothers has not been passed by congress.

3. Women have no choice but to work more and spend less time with their children.

Cathy's mom responds that the children who are neglected by their mothers will grow up and blame their mothers.

In the cartoon (dated 11-1-88), Andrea discusses how the next president will be appointing the Supreme Court Justices. Women and children are getting involved in the campaign because they don't want the Supreme Court to reverse the gains that have been made on affirmative action and abortion.

By the fall of 1990, things have changed slightly. Eight women are running for governor and eight for U.S. Senate. Of the nation's fifty governors, three are women. There are two women senators, and 28 women out of 435 members in the House.

Editor's Note
Originally, we planned to purchase the right to reprint the Cathy Cartoons. The price for the Cartoons was more than what the members of the Promethium Chapter of Iota Sigma Pi felt we could pay. Therefore it was decided to discuss the Cartoons, rather than reprint them.

6   **Entertaining**

J. P. Kilbourn

For the woman (working or otherwise) who wishes to entertain, I have just one bit of advice

K I S S

<u>K</u>eep <u>I</u>t <u>S</u>imple <u>S</u>ister

One way to **KISS** is to have a Pot Luck Party.

Pot lucks were not invented by husbands who felt guilty because they could not afford to take their wives out to dinner.

Pot Luck Parties were invented by women

-- who want to eat someone else's cooking

-- who want conversation and companionship

-- who want to show off their cooking abilities

-- who want a party and will share the effort to have one

Pot lucks are depicted in Jean Auel's *Clan of the Cave Bear* as happening among prehistoric peoples.

Other ideas for entertaining are:

1. eat in a restaurant.

2. eat a catered meal in your home.

3. support local foreign students by hiring them to prepare a native dish.

4. have a classic sit down dinner party where you do all the work and get all the credit.

5. have a theme party with prepared or purchased food.

Or, you can decide not to entertain. You can establish some new traditions and ways to celebrate the holidays so that one woman does not have all the responsibility of shopping, decorating and cooking.

Okay, so you are expected to entertain sometimes, but you do have the right to say "No" to the perfectionist type of entertaining that imposes on your time, property and disposition.

Jeanne Sullivan writes: For me, even when it's an exhausting day, it's a real ego trip to know I can be a "Superwoman" when I have to be and I know that I'm appreciated. Nobody really forces me to take on the extras--I do it by choice.

WHY DO YOU ENTERTAIN?

1. You genuinely enjoy entertaining.

© 1991 Ellen Quade, suggested by Carole Gatz,

2. You have a hidden agenda--For example, you want to accomplish something that can best be done in a situation you control.

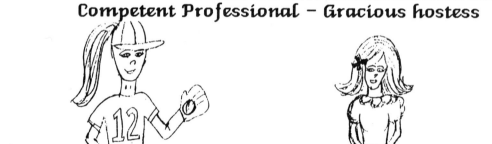

> *I will invite Joe so that he'll meet Susan, who would be perfect for his Systems Analyst Position.*
>
> © 1991 Virginia Lindley, suggested by Carole Gatz

3. Your business or profession requires it.

How you entertain depends on what you want to accomplish and the image you want to project. You can choose to be the competent professional or the gracious hostess.

Competent Professional – Gracious hostess

We'll meet at the park for a ball game and then have watermelon.

Please come to my house Friday night for cocktails.

© 1991 Darlene Angel

Page 52

4. Your spouse's business or profession requires it.

We often choose to help our husband's careers. How it should be done depends on the image we want to project. You can choose to be the competent helpmate versus gracious hostess.

Competent helpmate – Gracious hostess

We'll meet at the park for a ball game and then have watermelon.

Please come to my house Friday night for cocktails.

© 1991 James Angel

Entertaining at home is possible if you get help and cooperation from your housemates. An at-home pot-luck minimizes cooking time. With commercially prepared food, the outcome is usually predictable and requires less effort and planning. You can use a delicatessen or caterer if the extra expense is acceptable.

You must think about the time and effort to clean the house, decorate the table, and cleanup afterwards. Marsha Lakes Matyas suggests that you set the table the night before and cover it with a cloth. She advised that she did this before a Christmas Party and it worked.

Page 53

If having me pay the check is a threat to your masculinity, how does having me as your supervisor make you feel? I asked you, I get to pay!

© 1991 Virginia Lindley, suggested by Carole Gatz

Men and women follow the same rules for business entertaining. The person who invites the other person pays the bill, regardless of sex. Tell the waiter in advance who gets the bill, for either social or business meals.

Eating out means you don't have to do the dishes!

Entertaining doesn't always mean eating, it could mean going to the theater, a concert or a sporting event. It could mean chips and coke over a game of Scrabble.

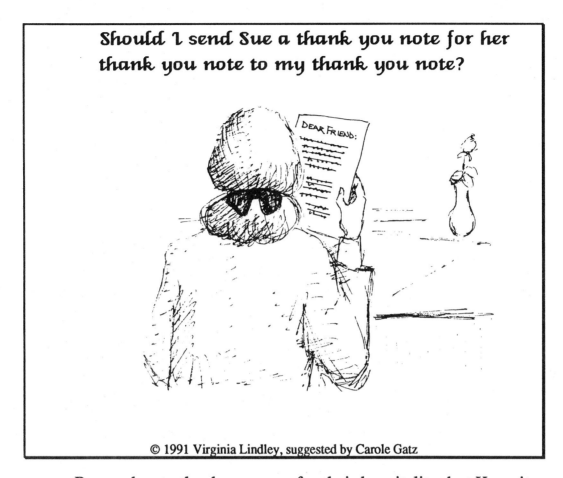

Should I send Sue a thank you note for her thank you note to my thank you note?

DEAR FRIEND:

© 1991 Virginia Lindley, suggested by Carole Gatz

Remember to thank someone for their hospitality, but Keep it Simple Sister (KISS).

7 Childcare

Sue Kohlhepp

As long as women continue to provide room and board for fetuses, women will have problems to solve and decisions to make that men do not. Pregnant working women encounter discrimination and pressure to either terminate the pregnancy or terminate the employment.

The Nurturing Network, founded by Mary Cunningham, is a nonprofit support service that helps working women and college students cope with unplanned pregnancies. There are many programs for pregnant teenagers but few are available for older working women. Pregnant women who are bankers, nurses, lawyers and administrative assistants have used Nurturing Network, which helps arrange for free housing, low cost medical care and, in many cases, temporary employment.

Nurturing Network has obtained some corporate support. According to an April 4, 1988 *Newsweek* article, more than 80 companies say they hire pregnant mothers for temporary jobs. But many companies are not supportive when one of their employees has a pregnancy that is inconvenient to the company, which is why legislation is needed to protect a woman's right to work while pregnant.

Here are some of the pressures married women are subject to:

1. Desperation for sons. Aminocentesis is a uterine test that can be used to determine the sex of an unborn child. In societies that value males more than females, amniocentesis leads to the aborting of female fetuses. This is a common practice among Chinese, East Indians, Koreans and other cultures.

2. Pressure to be a mother as well as a job-holder. Many women assume the dual burden of family and job.

In the United States, working women have statutory entitlement to job protection, maternity leave or health coverage for themselves and their newborn child. But new mothers may have to choose between leaving newborn infants with a caretaker before they themselves are physically ready to return to work, or losing their job.

"Modern Women's Dual Burden" by Judy Mann
   A review of "A Lesser Life - the Myth of Women's Liberation in America" by economist Sylvia Ann Hewlett.
   Hewlett's arguments and her book are bound to be controversial. She has provided a framework for a women's movement that will address the most pressing daily concerns of working women's lives. Women are 53 percent of the population and 44 percent of the work force; 90 percent of these workers will have children and "most of them have no option but to try to hang on to their jobs during their childbearing years," she writes. This, indeed, is the central dilemma of modern women's lives and she has faced it head-on.

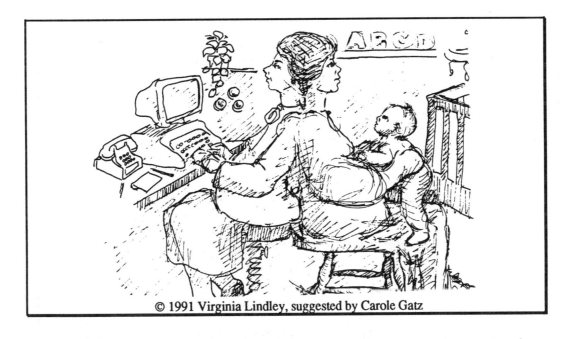

© 1991 Virginia Lindley, suggested by Carole Gatz

Women believe, their husbands believe, and society believes that women (not their husbands) are primarily responsible for the home.

Women who are full-time homemakers often feel that they are not as smart or as valued as women who work outside the home. Linda Burton, a mother from northern Virginia, who chooses to stay at home, has formed a group with three other northern Virginia women. They call themselves "Mothers at Home".

Linda feels that there are no role models for today's at-home mother, who may have a college degree, a number of years of work experience and an interest in maintaining her career skills while at home. Women who stay at home face extreme isolation because little attention is paid them by the media or by women who work outside the home. Mothers with careers have little time to spend outside their family.

Leslie Grow, another member of Mothers at Home, notes that there is a difference between baby-sitting and raising children. The home is a learning environment.

Society sends many conflicting messages about the importance of child care or women's work. Mothers at home often have to remind people that they do work, and they often have to try to be all things at all times.

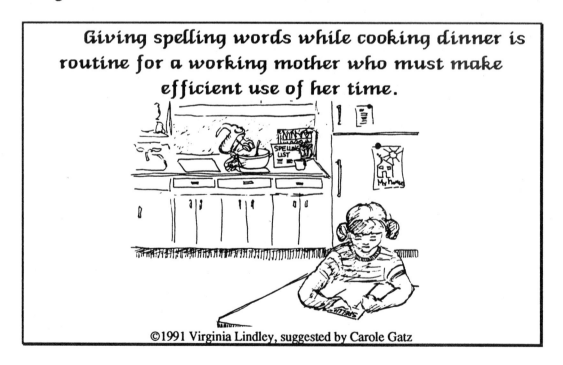

Giving spelling words while cooking dinner is routine for a working mother who must make efficient use of her time.

©1991 Virginia Lindley, suggested by Carole Gatz

Some parents try to schedule "quality time" because they see so little of their children.

"Quantity time," or a lot of time spent together, is not the most important factor in raising children. It doesn't take that long to fix two cups of hot chocolate. What it does take is the willingness to do it. Children should recognize that the parent wants to spend quality and quantity time with them.

You can set aside quality time every day. Set aside 15 minutes when you get home to discuss what happened during the day. Regardless of when the time is scheduled, both parent and child should want to take 15 minutes of uninterrupted time together.

The question of who cares for the children while parents work is still being debated in our society. In some families, a relative may be able to help. Some argue that employers or the government provide child care.

The National Association for the Education of Young Children (NAEYC) is a source for information on early childhood care and education for children, birth through age 8. Please contact the Information Service of NAEYC for the NAEYC's Catalogue and further information.

NAEYC
1834 Connecticut Ave. N. W.
Washington, D. C. 20009
1-202--232-8777

It will take all of us working together to overcome all the stereotypes and enable our children to grow to their fullest potential. This is a worthy goal for all peoples.

Men are not expected to be primary caretakers of children. Men are becoming aware that there are advantages to providing child care. If a father mentors his daughters, they will have a strong relationship. Women who have a strong bond with their fathers do better in the business world. Daughters can create their own identity separate from their fathers. Fathers can also mentor their sons. Sons who see their father, without the male stereotype that men can't show feelings become, as adults, better fathers themselves.

Dad, I need to tell you something – it is Father's day and all that and – well – uh – you know what I mean?

Yes, Son, the "I love you" is caught in your throat. It is all right, I understand.

© 1991 Virginia Lindley, suggested by J. P. Kilbourn

Careers and family can also be sequential. When children arrive, the mother or father stays home or works part time. Once the children are grown, the parent can make other arrangements.

Part-time work is ideal because it enables you to keep your skills up to date. You can advance toward career goals while working part time. Job sharing is where two people each work half working part time Job sharing is where two people each work half of a full time job. The employer benefits because one person can pinch-hit for the other. Also job-sharers are more productive because errands and doctor appointments are scheduled for their days off.

"Careers and Kids" by Edith Fierst

Young women will have to make up their own minds, based on their individual situation, whether these role models are the ones they can or want to follow. The answer will not be the same for everyone. But in considering the options before them, the young will surely want to take into account the experience of those who have managed to have both a family and a successful career by doing so sequentially.

© 1988 Ms Magazine

8 Coping with Teenagers

J. P. Kilbourn

I don't have all the answers but I do know some of the things that worked and some that didn't!

Children change a lot when they become adolescents and young adults. This changes the lives of their parents forever. Not only must the parents react differently toward their children, they must also react differently toward each other. The parents also must cope with other problems at the same time, such as the death or disabilities of their own parents. Women often go from the responsibility of caring for young children to the responsibility of caring for older parents, with no time for themselves.

When the children were small, the parents decided where their children would be at any given time. Adolescents should and do assume more control of their own lives, including:

> what they do for fun
> their friends
> where they spend their time
> their transportation
> when they come home at night

Problems arise if families are not able to change together. Teenagers want to gain control of their lives while parents want to retain control. A teenager exhibits irresponsible and/or rebellious behavior in an effort to control their own life. A parent (or parents) attempts to regain control because he or she does not trust their child. Or parents want teenagers to assume more responsibility while the child wants only the additional freedom.

Problems also arise if one parent decides that the teenagers can be trusted and the other parent feels that the teenager can not be trusted. Thus, parents give mixed signals! One parent is overly trusting and other is overly controlling. This happened in our family. Now the one parent is learning how to trust and the other parent is learning how to control less. The key seems to be to talk about it!

Francine Siegal suggests, in a newspaper article entitled "The struggle between parents and adolescents," that adolescents and parents should start preparing for adulthood early by sharing their concerns with each other. Parents state that they want to and will give more responsibility to their children if the children act responsibly. The parents use these criteria to measure responsibility:

1. Teenager does well in school and extracurricular activities - not necessarily "A's" or always being "First" but what is expected, given their abilities.

2. Teenager chooses responsible friends who share the schoolwork and other standards of the family.

3. Teenager does chores in a timely manner without needing more than an occasional reminder.

4. Teenager treats parents and other family members with respect.

5. Teenager is punctual and honest about activities such as when to expect them for dinner or if they are spending the night with a friend.

6. Teenager does not drink until the teenager is legally able to do so, and does not use illegal drugs.

7. Teenager follows family rules (such as length of time they can use the phone) and curfew times.

8. The family hears favorable comments from other parents, teachers, and family friends, about the behavior of the teenager when not at home.

© 1988 *Plain Talk* Column by Francine Siegal, M.D.

Teenagers can understand being evaluated and will accept criticism if they understand the reason behind it. It is all right if your children don't follow some suggestions. The aim is to teach adolescents how to make their own decisions and how to learn by their own mistakes.

As the mother of two college daughters I have lived through these teenage years. I am now at the stage of seeing them move from being children in my home, subject to my career, and my life style, to creating their own homes, their own careers, and their own life styles.

The hardest thing about this stage has been my loss of control, accepting that they may not do something the way I would do it, and that they are responsible for their own actions.

My daughters learned that it is all right to disagree with their mother. This has been as hard for them as for me. We do not agree on many things but they are responsible for their own beliefs.

It is harder to grow up and change in a world that is experiencing profound changes. These days, a woman has career expectations just as men have always had. But she also has marriage and family expectations. It is up to each of us to define what our expectations are. You can have it all; you must decide for yourself what "all" is.

9 How You Look

Mary Ryan-Hotchkiss

The heroic stories of people such as Louis Braille aside, most people would agree that we rely to an amazing extent on our eyes. It takes incredible compensation and adjustment to accomplish without sight what we do so easily with our eyes. If we are sighted, we come to rely on visual data and sometimes don't go beyond what our eyes tell us. We have to recognize that, like it or not, our appearance is a major avenue of communication with those around us who also rely on their eyes.

When I encounter someone for the first time, the one essential characteristic that I notice and remember is the person's sex. Sometimes I'm extremely uncomfortable until I identify which sex they are. Have you ever driven behind someone with soft, long, curly, blond hair, only to be embarrassed or surprised when you pass them and find out it's a man? This is probably an example of one area in which our society has more restrictive expectations for men than for women.

Are we, men or women, discriminated against because of our appearance? You bet! Are we stereotyped because of our appearance? Probably.

Imagine you're at your rural home, alone. You see someone in rumpled, raggedly clothes look up and down the road and then begin walking up your driveway. The person comes to the door. What do you think about before you open it? Do you hesitate to open the door?

Or imagine you're sitting outside a local school waiting to give a child a ride home after a special test. Someone taps on your window, and you turn to see a well manicured hand, a gold bracelet and a cashmere sweater. Do you open the door to see what they want? Or now you're driving along a remote country road and you see an attractive, well groomed and coiffed young person walking in the gravel in fine leather shoes.

That man looks mad – should I offer to help?

© 1991 Ellen Quade, suggested by Mary Ryan-Hotchkiss,

That woman looks mad – should I offer to help?

© 1991 Ellen Quade, suggested by Mary Ryan-Hotchkiss

Page 66

Do you stop to offer them a ride? In all of these cases, would it make a difference if the person were male or female? Possibly. Does it make a difference what their appearance is? Do we discriminate based on appearance? Unquestionably.

There are two main facets to our appearance: what we've been given, and what we do with it. <u>People are discriminated against because parts of their body are different from the norm.</u> While it may not be "right" and we may train our children not to stare or ask embarrassing questions, we nevertheless notice abnormality.

If we find ourselves in such a category, e.g. fat in a skinny community, or Caucasian in an oriental country, or female in a predominantly male workplace, it is to our best interest to make others comfortable with our differentness. We may choose to do that in a variety of ways.

First of all we have to recognize our differences. Next we may be able to show that it doesn't make a difference because it isn't an essential characteristic in this situation. A paraplegic can operate a computer as well as an athlete. We might be able to demonstrate that our differences are really an asset in this situation.

Everyone on this team is supposed to do rewiring, but since I'm smaller I can do the jobs that require getting into tight places.

© 1991 Virginia Lindley, suggested by Mary Ryan-Hotchkiss.

If we know that our differences do put us at a disadvantage, we need to recognize that too, and show how we compensate. "I know I may not be able to carry as many heavy boxes at one time as you do, but I'll just keep at it until I get them all taken care of." The effort here is to make it clear that appearance is just appearance and does not equate to total performance.

Nature gives some male birds brilliant plumage to attract females. Perhaps we use our clothes for the same purpose. It can be argued whether women array their plumage for men or for other women, but people do notice our clothes and sometimes act on the messages those clothes send. Advertising tells us many reasons for dressing a particular way. An ad for men's suits proclaimed

"The Executive Look, to show you've arrived."

A billboard in Tokyo suggested you should buy a certain brand to "Let people know who you are." Taking a different tack, an ad for an expensive, mod ski jacket said, "With a jacket like this people won't notice your skiing".

Some clothes give clear messages, such as the blouse with a large arrow pointing to the woman's abdomen.

©1991 Virginia Lindley, suggested by Mary Ryan-Hotchkiss

In fact, T-shirts proclaim where we've been, what we belong to, and what we dislike.

If we accept that our clothes, even without printed messages, are making a statement about ourselves, we need to think about what messages we want to send and the effect those messages may have, just as we think about what we say verbally to people. Perhaps the most difficult dilemma in dressing--and in life--is deciding what message we want to send. We may have early programming about who we are that we want to overcome. By sending out a particular message with our appearance, we can get feedback from those around us that can actually help us be who we want to be. Our appearance is a sign that says, "Treat me this way." Just be sure you know what you are asking for.

If we are different in a particular setting, for example, a woman in a predominantly male workplace, we may need to be especially thoughtful about our appearance. We could use our dress to convey our authority or position, or to emphasize our professionalism. We might choose to adopt the unofficial uniform of that workplace and dress as similarly as possible to our co-workers to make them comfortable with us.

I interviewed at a midwestern consumer products company in which every professional woman dressed in conservative blue or grey suit and a white blouse with a bow at the neck. I'm sure they were not ordered to wear such a uniform. They wore it to fit in and make their associates comfortable. One time, all three men in a meeting in my office were wearing the same type of blue dress shirt.

Before our daughter started high school, she was in an absolute tizzy. She looked all over town for the shoes and the pants and the sweaters that would give her just the right look. She thought she wanted to look different from her classmates. Each article was carefully selected to be unique. Taken all together, though, the look of those first day students was amazingly similar. A student who had worn clothes from the wrong era would have been noticed.

THANKS FOR READING AT THE BREAKFAST TABLE, SQUID FACE.

HAPPY TO, HONEY.

I believe that women are judged more on their appearance than men, but women are allowed more variety in colors and styles. Women's clothes, having more diversity, get noticed more. As adults, in business or social settings, we need to decide if we want to be noticed because of our clothes. Do we want our clothes to be so neutral that they blend in with the background, or do we want those clothes to be part of the message we project?

It is difficult to make a particular statement if we differ from the norm in sex or another essential characteristic such as size. People who are above or below average height or weight may not find appropriate items in stock. Often it is possible to find what you want if you're willing to pay for it. Busy people have a problem finding the time to shop. Some stores have personal shoppers who will assist you in putting together a wardrobe or ensemble. The fashion industry may not have our money in mind when they fill the stores with this year's look. Clothiers are in the business of making money, so we must vote with our feet and our pocketbooks.

What is a perfect figure? It has changed through the years from the more robust figures of Rubens to the anorexic, weight-watching style of today. Above all else, know yourself, and be true to yourself.

© 1991 Linda M. Reilly

Editor's Note
Lead Donuts are donut shaped objects made out of lead which are sometimes found in waterbaths in laboratories. They are not suitable for eating!

10 Put Downs

Sue Kohlhepp

Our society is rampant with women being put down by men.

> Women need to speak against dual standards
> by Dolores Curran
> Back in my early days of writing, the '50s and '60s, if I wrote a major article on a weighty subject such as a social issue, I was often asked by editors to use a pseudonym or my initials instead of my first name "so men will read it."
> © 1988 Catholic Sentinel

Men wouldn't read thought-provoking articles if they know the author is a woman. If she wrote humorous or family articles Curran could use her first name. I've heard it said that Anonymous was a woman because, if Anonymous was a man, he would have used his name.

Sometimes it seems that to be accepted by men, a woman must appear strong (but not too strong) and to be accepted by women, a woman must appear weak (but not too weak). Sometimes women are attacked for their femininity whenever they show strength. For example, if a woman has a strong, commanding voice, a man says, "she talks like a man." This description attacks her femininity.

Questions that trivialize a woman's statements are especially difficult to handle. Some men can not accept that women are able to reach beyond subjective experience while dealing with general issues. Some seem to think it's a man's right to ignore or plagiarize ideas simply because they originated with a woman.

The Rev. Annette Arnold-Boyd wrote the following letter: I guess I block a lot of stuff out. I know that's simply a convenient coping mechanism. For example, when I was looking for a chaplaincy position in the late '70's it took me a while to realize that whether it was in writing or verbal, when it was stated "the man will do this and the man will do that," that is what they meant and I might as well have been a green and purple rhino.

Strangers can be interesting. When I wear a black blouse with a clerical collar they often ask: "Are you a sister?" I politely say: "No, I'm an Episcopal Priest." Then they say: "Can you marry?" or "How did you decide to do that?" "What do you do?" (They always seem surprised that I do the same things as any other priest) or "The question I've always wanted to ask a priest is . . ." This can either be a serious matter or a curious question.

Several times I've been asked (including once by my chiropractor and another time by a very ill man in intensive care) "How do you keep your collar so white?"

Sometimes the questions are not so kind. When I was single, before I met my husband, I've been asked, generally by older lay people and clergy who opposed the ordination of women, "Couldn't you be happy with a husband and home?" So I'd answer that it seemed at the time that God didn't have that in mind for me. Yet I never did rule out the possibility.

Maybe this is something that is just peculiar to ordained women. When the church was debating the ordination issue and when I was in seminary (I don't hear it very often now, but it still surfaces from time to time) they will say something like: "The ordination of women caused me so much pain and grief." Recently, I wondered if those who felt so grieved also said that to get their way with their mothers or wives? Just a thought. It's like their saying everyone can be a Christian, except women who are ordained - they are in another category, certainly not human.

I was the first woman at Seabury-Western to play the 32 bell carillon, and the second or third to officiate a sung Evensong, and the first to be a thurifer (the person who swings the incense). I thought to be a thurifer would be fun, but I was put off the schedule many times because I was female. Then I'd go ask again. Finally, I was so persistent and it was near the very end of the year that a special service was scheduled so I could be thurifer. Guess what? A man was scheduled. I went to the man and told him he wasn't going to do it; he could do it next year. Then I went to the scheduling person to teach me how to be thurifer, whether he liked it or not.

I am not a strong person because of upbringing and/or by nature, but these kinds of things have made me stronger. I know one woman at seminary whose field education supervisor told her to meet him at his apartment at 8 p.m. for her evaluation. She told him that was totally inappropriate; and didn't get the good evaluation she deserved. We had a woman who should have received a highly prized preaching award. Rather than give it to her, the faculty didn't award the prize that year.

Over the years, I've noticed that women who appear weaker generally have an easier time in pursuing ordained ministry than older stronger-appearing women. But when the men learn a young, weaker-appearing woman is just as determined as an older, stronger women, the weaker woman loses her male support too. (The support that the males were giving wasn't really support in the first place.) The women learn they can do just fine, even better, without the male support.

When I celebrate the Eucharist or preach in a church that has not had a woman at the altar or pulpit before, there always seems to be someone who says in a somewhat surprised voice, "If a woman had to come, I'm glad it was you." Maybe they don't realize what a put down that is to women clergy.

That also shows the importance of the availability of women clergy. I think it is just a matter just of never having met a woman priest, and discovering that we really are okay people and are just as competent as men.

At a bus stop a few years ago, a man asked me if I was a woman minister. I said, "Yes." He said, "I'm glad, we have a woman minister at our church too." What a refreshing encounter that was!

The whole matter of woman and religion is personal, but do men realize how rude and offensive they are when they are introduced to me and will only shake hands with, talk to and look at my husband? The former Bishop of Chicago, Bishop Montgomery, was very much opposed to the ordination of women to the priesthood. Yet I have great respect for him, because I felt that he respected me and cared, and that makes a big difference when it comes to a professional relationship.

I think a lot of silence is used to suppress women. It's like ignore her and she'll go away. So when we pursue our careers we learn to be persistent and sometimes stronger than we thought.

Another avenue of suppression is a committee. (A committee) is used if the man doesn't want to commit to a decision about a woman's career because he doesn't want it publicly known he's opposed to her. I've seen a committee formed with its members chosen carefully, but stacked in opposition to the woman. There's no way a woman can get through this committee and it's best to choose another path to get to the same place. I've seen this happen with church vestries and vocation committees at both the parish and diocesan level.

In addition, there are those passive/aggressive men who have public and private opinions which are at the opposite ends of the poles. They will not stand firm on their conviction. They either elude the issue or talk to men one way and to women another. Or they talk to one group in support of and another group in opposition to the women's ordination issue. They have a way to always come out smelling like a rose (to themselves anyway).

Recently, I heard someone say that because half the students in seminary are women there is going to be a serious clergy shortage in a few years - because those women are going to have babies. When I was in seminary, some alumni came to visit. At breakfast one priest who sat next to me said, "You must have come to seminary to get a man." I answered, "No, that isn't what I had in mind." A while later he said, "Well, maybe you came to seminary to go into Christian Education." I said, "No, I don't think that quite fits me."

In conclusion I am happily married with a daughter in kindergarten, and find that continuing to pursue my career as a priest is challenging and rewarding.

How does one handle put downs, the double standard, attacks on femininity, trivializing one's statements, and plagiarism? The offenders need to know they are out of line. This reminder can be done with humor and grace, and without bitterness or accusations. You could point out that the speakers didn't realize the implications of their words and that they certainly wouldn't want to make such a mistake in the future. You are doing them a favor to point out how their actions are perceived by others.

Judy Blum-Anderson writes: In addition to finishing the last two chapters of my doctoral dissertation and managing a home for my family, I am also spending the year working several hours a week at an elementary school in order to obtain my principal's credentials. Since I am not employed by the school district in which I am working, I am able to control the amount of time that I spend working at the school. It was my choice to volunteer; I felt that it was the only way I could reach my professional goals and still have a husband and children who like me.

Unfortunately, I am the first person to go through the university administration program without being employed by a school district, and the men in charge of my administration program are suspicious of my motives. It is my goal to be able to manage my time efficiently; it was their belief that I am trying to get through their program by spending as little time as possible. They wanted to have a meeting to discuss my situation and the meeting was going to be held without me. Since I objected to being excluded from a meeting to decide my fate, I was included in the meeting.

The meeting was held in a room arranged like an amphitheater. The three male professors sat in the first tier of chairs. I was directed to a chair on the floor level--a chair one of the professors jokingly referred to as the "hot seat". Had I taken this chair, I would have been seated at a level below them looking up to them.

It was immediately obvious to me that sitting in this chair would put me at a psychological disadvantage and I decided to take control of the situation. I set my materials on a table and suggested that we all sit around the table. In order for me to maintain the level of confidence I needed to effectively argue my case, I had to avoid sitting in the "hot seat." The "hot seat" was no joke to me. My plan worked and this was a successful meeting for me.

Marjorie Enneking and Amy Mulnix write that after they gave what they felt were excellent, serious presentations, men told them how attractive they looked. The only suitable response is no response.

Sharon Dunwoody writes that she has experienced problems being a woman in the professor business but has chosen not to acknowledge them. She feels that there were no instances where gender has had a negative impact on her work life sufficient to warrant telling about it. All instances of discrimination, she felt, were relatively minor problems, situationally irritating with no long-term consequences.

> Women in Science by Daniel E. Koshland, Jr.
> The threat of a serious shortage of scientific personnel looms in the years ahead. . . Women are one conspicuously underrepresented group in the higher echelons of academia and industry. . . As the country expands into an ever increasing technological base, the need for women and minorities in both academia and industry increases proportionally. It may cost some money, some effort, and some understanding, but the voyage to full equality can be even more exciting and worthwhile than the voyage into space.
> © 1988 Science

Since there are real losses of scientific and other talent, discrimination based upon gender, costs us.

© 1991 Virginia Lindley, suggested by Sue Kohlhepp

© 1991 Virginia Lindley, suggested by Sue Kohlhepp

Page 80

Teachers and administrators in schools and universities need to be sensitive to the stress of the pressured student or the untenured teacher. The encouragement of a steady friend to keep trying and praise for work well done are crucial in building the self-confidence of a developing professional.

Words are important, but actions are more so. Programs to make it easier for women to continue their professional involvements during childbearing years are needed.

For example, several universities have introduced stop-the-clock programs that enable women raising children to have tenure decisions postponed.

Other universities have half-time appointments, or extend-the-clock programs. On-site, subsidized day care help working families.

It is o.k. for a man to teach less because he serves on editorial boards - a woman who teaches less to help raise a child is labeled as less than a full contributor.

Some ethnic groups are in situations similar to those of some professional women:

They have few role models.

They need special encouragement in hostile territory.

Encouraging women and minorities takes effort, understanding, and some money, but the resulting equality will be more beneficial than the space program.

Humor is the ability to look at a situation from a new point of view. Sometimes, we can laugh at ourselves and change our perspective on our lives.

We feel we must be gainfully employed to have worth. But men sometimes find themselves without a job. Women have felt important centering their lives around their home, husband and children. Men have made their jobs their lives; their career an indication of their worth as a human.

SYLVIA

by Nicole Hollander

11 Your Own Business

Angela Eggleston

There have been radical changes in our culture since Iota Sigma Pi was founded in 1902. At the turn of the century, a woman's success was in the success of her husband, children and extended family. It was unusual for a woman to look for achievement outside of the family circle.

Iota Sigma Pi served to promote the advancement of women in chemistry with recognition, awards, and the publication of a newsletter. Women had few role models to emulate, few mentors to promote them and few professional women with which to communicate. Over the years, Iota Sigma Pi has helped to bring women chemists together and to set up a network of support for women in chemistry.

Professional women now have colleagues in academics and in business. Still few in number, older women find few role models as they evolve from the professional employee to the professional employer.

Developing our leadership skills in academics or in business requires a shift from traditional roles. Women are taught to accept the surrogate rather than to accept the principal position. Our culture lets us know in numerous ways that it is not becoming to be bright, aggressive, competent, and independent. Perhaps we will someday succeed in our careers, yet give up little of our successes as wives and mothers. We have to learn to delegate responsibilities, accept constructive feedback and, above all else, accept our own competence and independence rather than apologize for our gifts.

Each woman must define her goals and the timetable for achieving of them. She learns from *Consumer Reports* which automobile meets her needs; she must distinguish the responsibilities that can be delegated from those that can't. She must manage both a full-time career and her personal life. She must evaluate objectives and achievements needs in an ongoing, continuous process.

Not all that a woman achieves as a professional is enviable. You may have your ego stroked and not have to be responsible for some duties, but you lose your extra time. You may strain your relationships with your family. You still need the support, admiration and respect of those who are near and dear. You may have to redefine your relationships. Thus, you will find that your growth is as stressful as it is fulfilling.

MOTIVATION

How do you evolve from being employed by someone else or being a mother to having another full time career?

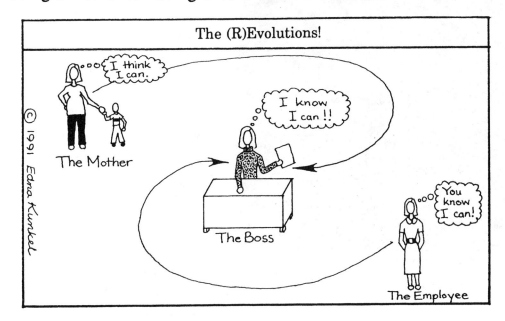

First, you have to want to! You must have the desire to be in business for yourself.

Second, you have to find an existing need and want to fill that need. One way of getting started is to send out a market survey or questionnaire to your prospective accounts.

    1) If you don't get any interest, it may not be the right time for you to start a business.

    2) If you do get a response, you can "run with it."

    3) If you get a minimum response, you should reconsider if you want to start your business.

TYPE OF BUSINESS AND CAPITALIZATION

Professional Package Contents: One unofficial uniform
©1991 Edna M. Kunkel

How do you determine what you want to do and how do you get funding?

A successful scientist who wants to start her own business needs to have a well-organized, long-term plan.

Women, as a group, are not taught how to package their business skills. Women generally are not taken as seriously (on a professional level) as men. These problems are solved if you are aware of the expected professional package and by taking yourself seriously.

Along with being a qualified professional, you must present yourself in a manner that breeds respect and confidence.

The successful scientist who thinks of starting her own business needs to proceed according to a well-organized plan. Most scientists have considerable ability in their field and one or more related fields. Your first task is to define your marketable skills: what someone will pay you legally to do.

Then you should survey to find out if there is an existing need for your skills in the business community. Frequently, your most marketable talents or skills are not those which you would list first as your major strengths. For instance, a biochemist might find her experience in statistical analysis and computers more marketable. Her biochemistry may need to take a back seat for a while.

Once you have opened shop, your success or failure depends on the quality of your product or service and your ability to work within the client guidelines.

You must decide the most fruitful way to promote your new business.

Last but not least, you must analyze the competition to determine if there is room for your new venture. If there is substantial competition you have two choices:

1) challenge the existing competition because you think you can deliver a better product or service.

2) redefine your market.

You can analyze your market yourself or you can hire a professional marketing firm

The harder you work, the better your business will do. In essence, you are the mistress of your own fate.

DEFINE ONE'S MARKETABLE SKILLS

One way of defining your marketable skills is to prepare a resume. By listing what you have done as though you were applying for a job, you should get a picture of your marketable skills.

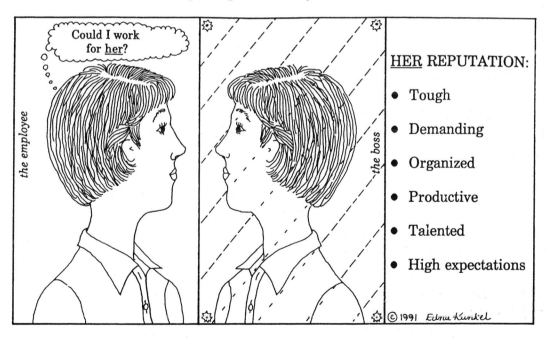

Mirror Image

The next step is to identify what you would like to do in your new business. You are both the employer and employee. You want yourself to be a satisfied employee who enjoys her work.

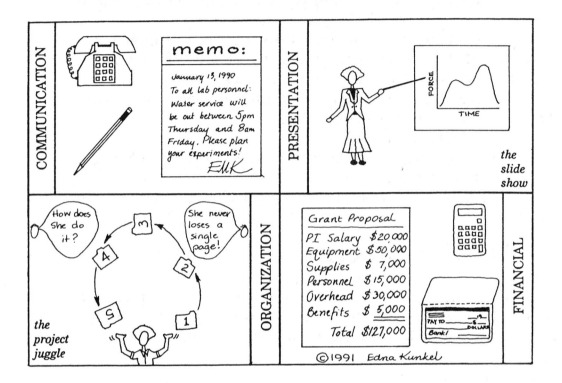

MARKETING

Next, determine how to package your service or product to attract potential buyers. You should decide how to promotion your business.

Here are three suggested promotions:

1) Prepare a brochure outlining your services and products. Address why they are worth purchasing and what problems you can solve for the customer. Use these brochures as direct-mail advertising to a select audience.

2) Write a monthly newsletter and send it to potential clients. Indicate what your services are and, as you get clients, indicate what you accomplished for them.

3) Send a press release to your local business journal about your business.

Page 88

KNOW YOUR COMPETITION

Know your competition. Is there room for a new business? Will you offer a unique service or product which will answer a specific need? Is there a special niche for you to fill? Also, is your service or product unique enough that it cannot be stolen by the competition?

CAPITALIZATION

Once you have an overall concept of the economic environment of your embryonic business, you must develop a financial projection. This financial projection is called a "pro forma." It quantitates the best guess of the business' cash flow and, therefore, its capital needs for the first twelve months.

An extended pro forma includes a five-year projection summary, taking into consideration the changing competition of the marketplace. Consider inflation, business expansion, and day-to-day operating costs (i.e. overhead).

The information needed by a bank to evaluate loan request includes:

      1. A description of your business and its operation.

2. A description of the experience and management capabilities (including a complete personal resume of each principal) that will make your business a success.

3. A cash equity evaluation of the amount you will invest without borrowing.

4. An estimate of the value of the collateral you have available to support the loan.

5. A copy of the financial statement, including a balance sheet and income statement for an existing business, or a projection of your income, expenses, and profit for at least a full year of operation.

6. An itemization of the usage of the loan funds, projection of operating capital, accumulation of accounts receivable, expenses for equipment, machinery, remodeling, etc.

7. A personal financial statement from the owner, each partner, or each stockholder owning 20% or more of the business.

PREPARING A "PRO FORMA"

The first step is to conservatively estimate the revenue you expect to generate in the first twelve months. Revenue may come from grants or contracts (either business or governmental), from the sale of services, or from the sale of products. The estimate must be refined by using all of the information and the best information you have available to you.

The second step is to generously estimate the expenses you expect to incur during the first twelve months. You begin by taking into account any funds needed for the capital items of furniture and fixtures, machinery and equipment and building or leasehold improvements. Then you account for utilities, supplies, personnel, taxes and so forth.

When you have completed these first two steps you have created (in accounting vocabulary) a "pro forma", that is to say, a financial picture of your new business as if it had been in business for twelve months. Most small entrepreneurs miss this most critical evaluation of the financial needs of their business. If the first two steps are done correctly, the remainder of the capitalization process will fall into place.

After you have formally written your estimate of revenue and expenses, you then look at the timing of the inflow and outflow of cash - a funds-flow analysis. Always estimate inflow conservatively and outflow generously.

Now you begin to develop an accounting picture of the amount of capital you will need to stay in business. You will have to guess when your input of funds will begin to match your output. You may find (to your dismay) that these will not match each other in the first year, this is often the case. If planned properly, this early mismatch need not discourage your venture.

If you need to approach investors for money, you will need to present your "pro forma" in the proper format. An accountant can help write the formal papers, but if you work out many of the figures beforehand, you can keep your accountant's fees down.

You have completed all of the steps necessary to present your business systematically to others. You now need to dynamically and convincingly solicit support. There are many places to obtain the funds. You may go to investors who know your work and who will invest in your business. The Small Business Administration may supply the funds. You may procure the needed funds from lending institutions, government loans, grants or contracts, or other scientific enterprises such as the pharmaceutical industry. You will search for still others. Once this selling job is complete, you are ready to start your new venture.

DATA SYSTEMS - Technical and Financial

The data system that you install should have two very distinct functions: a product function and an accounting function. Both should be taken into account when you purchase a manual or automated system. If you decide on a manual system, your investment requires less capital and is, therefore a less final decision. Manual data systems are labor intensive.

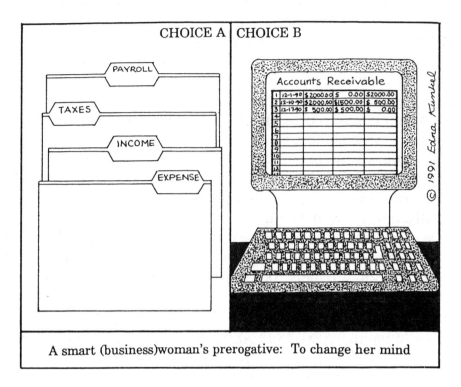

A smart (business)woman's prerogative: To change her mind

We all know we can manually collect and sort scientific data. The same sort of thing can be done with your accounting data. Labor is not inexpensive in the U.S.A.! If you think it is more reasonable to expend time rather than money as you start your business, then you should start by using established manual data systems.

Your technical data must be entered and processed against standard values. The obtained result must be communicated to the business requesting it.

You have several accounting functions to address, including:

    1. cost accounting, to satisfy your investors;

    2. agency accounting, if you are dealing with grants and contracts;

    3. and tax accounting, to satisfy the Internal Revenue Service.

Accounting data is the same in all these cases but how it is sorted depends on the desired outcome.

If you decide to use manual accounting, the One-Wright Cash Receipts and Cash Disbursements System is the most efficient. The One-Wright System is briefly described below.

Each account that you invoice has a separate card on which the amount owed is written. When payment is received, the amount of the payment is entered on the card in such a manner that the receipt is copied through onto a columnar spread sheet that is placed beneath the card. In this manner each account balance is kept current and all cash receipts are also accounted for on the spread sheet.

The cash disbursement system works the same way. Checks are made to overlay a columnar spread sheet. When each cash disbursement is written it produces a copy on the spread sheet. The amount of the disbursement can then be categorized into expenses, such as utilities, payroll, supplies and so forth. The totals of all disbursements and categories of disbursements are totaled each month. The twelve monthly spread sheets of both cash receipts and cash disbursements can then be used for yearly accounting.

If you have the capital to start with automated data systems, you will need to purchase a computer and software. I recommend the IBM AT or XT. This is a sound business computer and is supported by an excellent library of software packages. I also recommend the Sorcim/IUS micro computer software accounting packages. The general ledger package is the only software needed. Technical data needs can be accomplished with one or more software packages such as dBase III, Lotus 1,2,3 or technical data micro software. Written documents can be produced efficiently with WordPerfect 5.1 software.

If you choose a manual accounting system, a sales person will help you set up the system. Alternatively, you need someone to help program the software to your specific needs. If correctly programmed, a computer can be set up to produce cost, financial and tax accounting (information). Just as you need a chemist to evaluate the technical output, you need the services of a competent accountant to evaluate and translate the accounting data into final form and into the proper accounting format.

SYSTEMATIC EVALUATION OF THE GOING CONCERN

Your business venture has made progress along its scheduled path. You have been prudent in choosing a business that is marketable, sufficient capital has been acquired that there are funds available until the business reaches the time when income exceeds expenses, and you have installed data systems that will enable you to produce both technical and accounting information. The management of your going concern is somewhat different than management of embryonic (Ad)venture was.

A going concern needs planned and relatively steady growth in order to stay in business. The same skills that you used to evaluate the type of business you entered are now used to keep your business out of management, technical and financial trouble. Those technical skills developed in your professional career will easily translate to your business career. Management and financial skills now need to be developed or improved.

Management is a learned skill for most of us. It is important to find the time now to start learning better management skills by using of the abundant literature or by studying at a college or at management seminars. Good management requires a knowledge of human needs and relationships in the work place, motivation skills, and an understanding of your management style and how these impact on your employees. This awareness gives you the opportunity to approach problems that arise in a logical, constructive fashion.

The financial skills that you learned when you developed a financial projection (pro forma) formed a good basis for those skills that will be needed to oversee a going concern. You continue to project the business flow of income and expenses (cash flow) twelve or more months into the future.

You also search for ways to achieve controlled expansion. There will be times when opportunity offers exciting business growth. You must weigh the risks and the rewards. There will be other times when your business is sluggish and all your creative financial skills will be called upon to turn things around. Again, I suggest formal education to improve financial skills. Formal business education is efficient and not expensive. A multitude of seminars and academic courses are available.

You are on your way. You should continue to communicate with professional women colleagues in academics and in business. Be aware that you are now among those few who are the role models for other women.

12 Hitting Glass Ceiling

Carol Mount

We now present two successful women-owned laboratory businesses. These women went through the glass ceiling-the invisible barrier that keeps women from rising to the ranks of executive or full-professor.

Somewhere over the glass ceiling, she finds that the sky's the limit.

The first story is by Carol Mount on her business.

After several years of working in commercial and hospital laboratories, I decided it was time for a change. Luckily, the business I chose did not require a large initial outlay of capital to get started. My formal education for this new venture was a two day workshop sponsored by the Small Business Administration. I listened to statistics about low success rates for new businesses, but still was excited about starting my own company, a sole proprietorship.

I was familiar with a health screening program operated by an Eastern reference laboratory and decided to expand on this concept, concentrating my efforts on rural Midwest communities. My objective was to offer preventive health testing, a blood chemistry/hematology profile, in geographic areas that did not have local hospitals or labs.

My initial contacts in the communities were with the local physicians, whose support and approval were required to conduct the screening program. They would receive the lab results about their patients and were asked to report to the patient, via a postcard, their overall impression of these test results.

With their approval lined up, I then approached local civic organizations to help advertise the testing dates, to locate a building for the blood drawing and to help staff the drawing site. A bulk mailing was then sent to explain the program and announce the testing dates to the local residents.

The premise of the program was to establish baseline normal and individual values for the chemistry and hematology tests, and to repeat the testing annually. Therefore, if an individual became ill, normal values for these tests would already be available. In addition to the blood chemistry work, blood pressure and weight checks as well as glaucoma screens were often included.

The blood was drawn early on Saturday mornings (fasting specimen required) and the tests were performed within a few hours by a Midwest reference laboratory. Results were back to the patient's physician within 3-5 days. The physician in turn evaluated the results and notified the patient with his/her interpretation. We spent two consecutive Saturdays in each town, and returned annually. The testing was totally voluntary, and often entire families participated. The participants paid for the testing on site. In each town, the program grew as we established our professional reputation.

Although the program stressed preventive medicine, the lab results uncovered several individuals with previously unidentified elevated levels of glucose, triglyceride and cholesterol, and several women with low iron and hemoglobin levels. Many of these people became our best advertisement: they came back the following year to relate how the identification of an abnormal result allowed their physician to pursue the problem and initiate corrective therapy with the end result of a person who physically felt better.

The program grew annually in each town, and our phlebotomy team drew samples on as many as 300 participants in two hours. Within 3 years, there were 25 communities involved in the program, which kept us busy every weekend. Half of the fee paid covered the cost of testing; the other half paid the costs of advertising, postage, wages (phlebotomist) and equipment (table-top centrifuges and hematology rotators). I had an office in my home, so I had no office rental or other overhead. In addition to the trips to the towns for the actual blood drawing, I made several trips to speak with their local physicians and made slide presentations at civic club meetings to promote the program. My actual time involvement with the program averaged 3 days per week. I also contracted with private laboratories in my hometown to do their nursing home phlebotomy.

This business did not make me wealthy, but after 3 years of operation, a professional acquaintance approached me to buy the business. He was interested in building on the reputation and goodwill of the program and expanding it. I took this as my cue to sell, and we were able to agree on a price - not an easy task for a service-related business. I am now again an employee, but I count the 3 years with the program as a most educational and rewarding experience.

The second women-owned business is Consulting Clinical and Microbiological Laboratory, Inc. (CCML). It was incorporated in January, 1984 by microbiologist J. P. Kilbourn, who is also a registered medical technologist. Its initial purpose was to provide rapid turn-around-time on all clinical laboratory tests, especially microbiological ones. After a year of losing money, Kilbourn bought out her partner, changed the focus of the laboratory to just microbiology, and emphasized contract research.

This change has worked and Kilbourn now earns a comfortable salary working 40 to 60 hours a week. She has published articles on some of the contract research which has been performed by CCML. One key to the success of CCML was learning how to prepare professional service agreements and get them signed.

There are four basic parts to a Professional Service Agreement:

1. Subject matter
2. Payment
    a. How much
    b. When paid
3. Length of the agreement
4. Termination provisions

The Section Titles used in the Professional Services Agreement for the CCML are:

1. Research. Outline exactly what should be done and how long each step in the contract research project should take.

2. Payment. Explain the amount to be paid and billing process. Include provisions for expanding the research and list an hourly rate fee schedule as well as the out-of-pocket expenses which the client will be asked to pay.

3. Length of Agreement. Give an ending date for the research but include a provision for an extension. Indicate how the agreement could be terminated, and how payment would be calculated if the agreement is terminated early.

4. Proprietary Rights. If a marketable product or service results from the research a provision is included for CCML to obtain 1% royalty on the product or service.

The final line, above the signature of the President of CCML, for the signature and title of the person who authorizes CCML to begin the research upon receipt of the signed agreement.

Other things which might be included in a Professional Services Agreement include:

Background information,
Discussion of outside influences on the Agreement, and
Qualifications of the professional staff.

13 Hole in Glass Ceiling

J. P. Kilbourn

Joan Beck wrote an editorial "Hole in Glass Ceiling" which appeared in *The Sunday Oregonian.* (May 27, 1990). Beck discussed Ann B. Hopkins' six-year sex discrimination case against Price Waterhouse (a large accounting firm). Beck reports that a federal district judge in Washington had ordered Price Waterhouse to give Hopkins the partnership she wanted by the first of July.

Beck began her editorial by stating that Hopkins won a significant victory for the cause of women's rights and equal opportunity in the higher levels of corporate American. The win is not limited to corporate America. It is also a win for academic America. In both corporate and academic American, a clubby old-boy network has existed which excludes women and minorities by means of partnership rules, tenureship committees and other exclusionary strategies.

The Supreme Court ruled in 1984 that a law firm could be sued by an associate who was rejected for partnership. The plaintiffs must show some evidence of discrimination, but the employers need not present clear and convincing evidence that they acted in a non-discriminatory way. The employers need only show a preponderance of evidence to justify their actions.

Hopkins has been told she would have a better shot at a partnership if she walked and talked more femininely, had her hair styled, and wore more jewelry and makeup.

Woman gets partnership 7 years late
by Aaron Epstein

Ann Hopkins advised: I've got no problems with the way I walk, no problems with the way I talk, I don't wear makeup because, one, I'm allergic to it and, two, I wear trifocals, and I can't see to put it on with my glasses, and I can't see to put it on without my glasses.

© 1990 Knight-Ridder News Service

A CASE OF AN IRRATIONAL INEQUALITY $X \neq X$	
Name: M. J. Worker	**Name:** M. J. Worker
Height: 5'6"	**Height:** 5'6"
Weight: 130 lbs.	**Weight:** 130 lbs.
GPA: 3.75/4.00	**GPA:** 3.75/4.00
Age: 35	**Age:** 35
SS#: 123-45-6789	**SS#:** 123-45-6789
Years of Experience: 12	**Years of Experience:** 12

© 1991 Edna Kunkel

Women and minorities have often felt they were rejected as partner because they were not white and male. Hopefully, now a woman or a minority will learn the criteria for promotion and fulfill them. If women and minorities are able to network and mentor, they can help their younger colleagues obtain a coveted promotion.

For example, Martha Thompson, points out that there are three areas that are scrutinized for promotion at the Oregon Health Sciences University:

1. Scholarly activity
2. Teaching
3. Service

Scholarly activity involves

a. obtaining grants to perform research
b. performing research
c. publishing research papers
d. attending meetings
e. presenting papers at meetings
f. chairing sessions at meetings

Teaching includes managing a class of male students. Male teachers may develop a rapport with their male students. they may then ignore his poor teaching. Women and minorities have more difficulty developing rapport. Male students may unconsciously challenge a female teacher to see whether she can take the heat.

Taking the heat

If you want to find out how much teaching is required and how much emphasis is placed on teaching ability, talk to a sympathetic member of the Rank and Tenure Committee. If little value is placed on teaching and more on research, then you may want to emphasize the research over teaching.

"Service" is a term loosely applied to University Committee assignments. Again you should talk to a sympathetic member of the Rank and Tenure Committee to find out how much service is needed.

Rank and Tenure Committee minutes

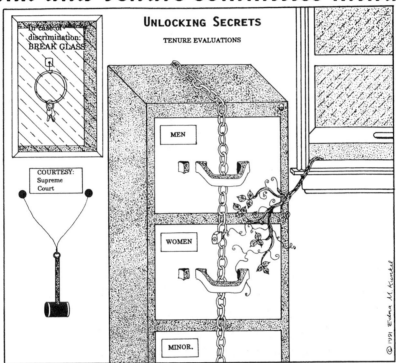

Women are often asked to serve on university committees. They accept because they are flattered by the request. But university committees take time away from research and teaching and are not given much weight when the candidate's resume is reviewed for promotion and/or tenure. Be cautious about which university committee assignment you accept if the assignment affects your available time for research and teaching. Ask the questions: How important is this university committee? What am I trading?

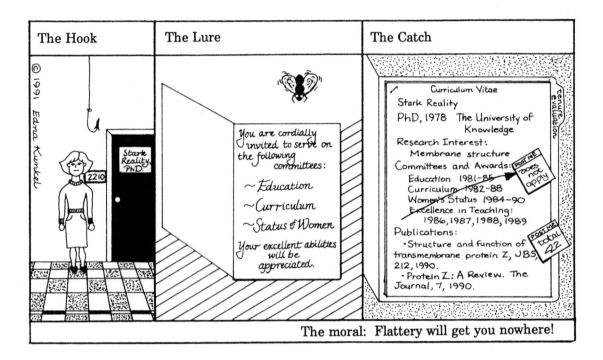

The Hook	The Lure	The Catch

The moral: Flattery will get you nowhere!

In interviewing Ph.D. astronomer, Lidia M. Crosa, who is working for her Ph.D. microbiologist husband as a research associate, I learned several things. First, Lidia felt her husband had as much trouble as a woman because he was a foreigner. Second, she felt her husband had succeeded because of the following traits:

1. He was confident about his abilities and assertive
2. He presented the best information in his resume
3. He tailored his resume to what the Rank and Tenure Committee felt was important.
4. He refrained from intentionally antagonizing a member of the Rank and Tenure Committee, yet he didn't try to be someone else.

14 Women in Academia

Lidia Crosa

It is the usual problem: career, family, or what? I think I have chosen the "or what" alternative. It may sound weird that, being an astronomer, I have been working in microbiology for the past nine years. How did it happen?

From very early in my life I wanted to be a scientist and to unravel the secrets of nature. Atoms seemed to be the right place to start. So, while still in my native country, Argentina, I went to college to study physics. It was not an easy start, since for the first year I had to fight with my father, a kind of old-fashioned Italian, who considered that physics was not a very feminine career.

Shatter the image, not the DREAM!

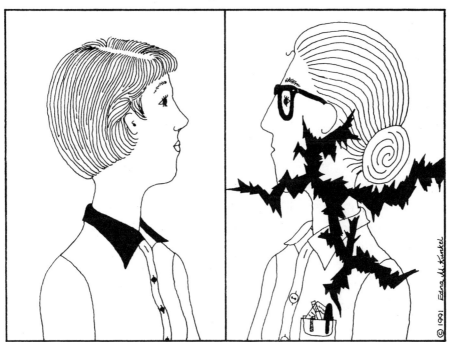

I was already an elementary school teacher (at that time it was possible to attend specialized high schools to get the degree). According to him, that was not only enough but it was the best profession for a woman, and I could start immediately earning the money I needed.

With my mother's encouragement (and the secret pride of my father), I obtained my undergraduate degree in physics, while tutoring and working as a science teacher in private schools.

At that point, I had my first specialty crisis: I liked many branches of physics.

Now that I've found the right tree . . . which branch do I climb?

©1991 Edna Kunkel

Biophysics was exciting. For one year I worked in a microbiology institute doing molecular research in living systems. During the same period I got married and my husband, a graduate chemist, went into microbiology. But my research was not progressing as I wished, mainly due to my inexperience and lack of guidance. For fun I took an astronomy course. I discovered a new exciting universe ahead of me and, since there was a good research group working in my university, I decided to join it.

During this time of indecision, my husband worked very hard and was able to obtain his Ph.D. in microbiology. We both applied for fellowships to continue our respective work in the U.S.A. I worked for one year at the Naval Research Laboratory on the east coast, but my husband's research group relocated to the west coast.

For a few months I continued to work in Washington D.C. and my husband worked in Seattle, but we both felt miserable being so far apart. So I moved to Seattle and decided to finish my Ph.D. in astronomy at the University of Washington.

Halfway through my graduate student life we had our first child, and near the end of my studies we had the second one. Life became even more complex. I struggled to find good, but inexpensive, daycare centers, took the babies to my classes or to my office while I was working, tried alternative schedules with my husband and other creative approaches. We had the good luck that, for a few months at a time, my mother or my husband's mother were able to come from Argentina to help us.

The next crisis came after obtaining my degree. It was difficult to find good jobs for both of us simultaneously. One thing was clear; whatever we planned to do in the future had to be done as a whole family. Now, to do work as an astronomer, I should have spent long stretches of time going to different observatories. Every time I had to do it I suffered. It was then that my husband had a good offer of a position in Portland, Oregon. We loved the northwest. But what about my career? There was no astronomy research anywhere around Portland.

We moved anyway, and I was able to obtain interesting positions teaching astronomy and physics in local community colleges. Simultaneously, I was helping my husband with his new laboratory. My old memories of biophysics were coming back, and I was having fun with the microbiology research.

Another child came. I kept running all the time between different locations. I realized that I could not do everything. I had to choose between my teaching jobs and the laboratory job. I liked teaching. Moreover, I liked teaching physics and astronomy, and I could envision projects to popularize science and bring more science to the community. But, I missed research.

Fortunately, I enjoyed the microbiology research and I also considered my work a contribution to the "family business." Possibly, working with my husband implied losing part of my independence as well as having to learn a lot about my relatively new field. However, considering how hard it is to obtain funding for research, keep an academic position and at the same time devote some time to a spouse and children, being a research associate in microbiology was not such a very bad deal. As a matter of fact, it was very satisfying!

And that is why I am still doing microbiology although I am an astronomer. Maybe someday I'll bring both subjects together working in another world.

A woman professor in a university anonymously responded as follows when asked to comment on appointment, promotion and tenure:

There was nothing in my formative years in my family or origin, or in my life as a woman, that prepared me for the gamesmanship of the academic world. But somehow I seem to have arrived and have done well with most of the game. Let me summarize my experience and what I mean by that statement.

I was born in 1938 and, even though my parents never had a college education, four out of six of their children finished college. Being the fifth child in line, I was well programmed to go to college in 1956, even when only 10% of the high school graduating females went on to school, and everyone "knew" that it was to obtain an MRS degree. Fortunately I was bright and was a serious and conscientious student in high school so I was well prepared for the rigors of a college education.

In 1956 the major acceptable degree options for women were: education, nursing, and secretarial science. Even though I could have become a nurse through a three-year diploma training program through a hospital, I knew I wanted to go to college. So I entered a baccalaureate nursing program (one of the few in those days) and graduated in 1960. Even while in undergraduate school, I told myself that I should go "all the way" and get a Ph. D. right away. But like many young women of that era, I married young, age 21, and had two children fairly soon. For the next 5 years of my life, I worked as a nurse, supported my husband who was in graduate school, and took care of my family. When my youngest child was old enough to leave in care of someone else, I enrolled in a masters graduate program and my husband went to work to support us.

I knew then that I did not want to be a staff nurse and pound the cement in a hospital all my life. I did well in graduate school and began thinking that teaching or administration was my better suit. For the next 11 years following my masters degree, I tried both nursing education and nursing administration positions (while my husband returned to school for his final degree). It was clear to me that nursing education would be the better choice for my future career.

In 1976, I entered a doctoral program at a major university. At the time of my decision, there were only 5 Ph.D. programs in nursing across the United States, none of which were in my home town. At the time of my decision, it felt like I did not have the option of going out of my home town for a Ph.D., so I obtained my Ph.D. at the local University in an allied area; education. Educational psychology, higher education and business administration were fields that would be useful in my goals in nursing education. Again my husband and I leap frogged during these years with him working while I was going to school, and vice versa.

My academic career began before I obtained my Ph.D. In the clinical sciences, such as nursing, it is common for nurses in leadership positions to have adjunct or clinical appointments (unsalaried usually) in their local schools of nursing. I began with such positions at a major university. Then I joined a faculty at a private university's school of nursing for a couple of years.

I was a good teacher and came by these skills naturally, but I never had anyone take me under their wing and teach me the ropes.

The MENTOR: intellectual shareware?

©1990 Edna M. Kunkel

Most of what I learned about working in an academic workplace was experiential but since the early faculty positions were junior faculty and non-tenure track positions, I was not a threat to anyone so I was not vulnerable. I stayed on one year beyond my Ph.D. to do a year's post-doctoral work with one of the first post-doctoral programs in nursing in the USA. This was during the academic year of 1980-1981. Though this did not constitute a full fledged faculty position, it served as valuable time for me to catch my breath after the Ph.D. and start some research and writing. I wish I had stayed two years instead.

I was learning a lot about academic politics through my husband's experience. He was on a fixed term appointment and could not receive tenure because of the institutional politics in a cutthroat research institution. I somehow knew that I would have to play it differently than he and instead of focusing on teaching, I would have to jump through other hoops if I were to become a full tenured professor some day. Thanks to one of my doctoral faculty (who came as close to a mentor as I would ever have), I learned that I

Page 110

should negotiate salary and rank in any position before I accepted my next faculty job and that one did not get anything unless they asked. I negotiated my first tenure track position as an associate untenured faculty in 1981.

① *The Approach.*
② *The Jump.*
③ *The Landing.*

TENURE

Committee

9.5 9.7 9.0

©1991 Edna Kunkel

The Academic Olympics: The Vault to Success

Since nurse faculty with Ph.D.'s were rare, and I had considerable nursing experience in my background, this negotiation was not difficult. During the three years that I was at this university, I went from a new Ph.D. to having literally a national reputation in nursing. This was largely because of my focus on writing and research in a new field and the energy I put into professional organizations. By the end of three years I received tenure at this major university, and I am sure it was because of my ability to bring in funding for research, and the publications I had written.

In 1984, my new national reputation put me in a position of being sought for leadership positions. When I decided to move from one university to another, at the suggestion of my mentor again, I negotiated a tenured track position as a full professor. I refused to move and take the new position without it. This was granted. So within five years of receiving my Ph.D., I went from an assistant professor to a full professor. I think the only reasons that this was possible were that:

     1. Ph.D. faculty in nursing were rare, so it was a supply and demand situation.

     2. My considerable experience and accomplishments before obtaining a Ph.D. lent themselves to meeting the requirements (i.e. publications in particular).

     3. My mentor taught me to negotiate for the best position I could get.

     4. My children were out of the home enabling me to work long and hard hours.

     5. My husband was an academician so he understood.

     6. I was willing to make physical relocations to be able to move ahead.

Sometimes one simply has to leave "home" or one school to be viewed with higher esteem by another school. Leaving one set of politics in one school and going to another school to start over has its advantages.

All in all, the academic role fits and suits me well. Since my husband is also a college professor, the role is really an integral part of our family life. In addition to the teaching, scholarly activities (research and publication) and community service missions of my job, I also maintain an active clinical practice on a part time basis. I would have to say that promotion and tenure have not been a problem to me during my career.

What has been a problem are the politics played within academia and within the discipline of nursing itself. Nursing has caring and nurturing as part of its historical base. When nursing grew into an advanced field and started emphasizing theory and research as other sciences had done years before, it became competitive and striving. How much of this was due to the fact that it is largely a female profession or due to being an immature profession, I cannot determine.

In our efforts to be as good as other scientific disciplines, we have lost a lot of the caring we used to do for each other and for our students. One can be a super teacher of students and not be able to jump through the hoops for promotion and tenure. Also the other health care professions do not always recognize nursing as a full-fledged professional and academic field. Therefore, being a Ph.D.

nurse and conducting research has not received a lot of credibility from the medical world in general and physicians in particular.

Because nursing entered the main stream of academia as the new kid on the block, we have had to work harder and longer than some of the other mainstreamed science disciplines. So, in some ways the promotion and tenure game is easier in nursing, but in other ways nursing is harder.

Promotion and tenure are not the biggest difficulties I have had personally. Rather the difficulty is the politics that lay all around in most academic systems. The focus on competition and success at any price has left me scarred. Backstabbing, professional jealousy, internal destructive dynamics, the "in people versus the out people", and other such games have been severe teachers for a politically naive kind of person like myself.

Honesty and integrity sometimes get lost in this setting. Perhaps I spent more energy trying to produce rather than paying attention to the group process issues and the interpersonal dynamics issues, causing me to learn the lessons the hard way. Power and prestige are things that people vie for in these settings and one has got to be able to "go for the jugular" at times.

If I were to advise a new Ph.D. coming into the field, I would suggest that

      1. You should learn the promotion and tenure guidelines as soon as possible and focus on meeting those criteria in the first couple of years in the setting.

      2. Attach yourself to someone who is able to protect and mentor you through the system.

      3. You should take time out to learn the social culture of your group.

Women, particularly in academia, do not have a history of mentorship. More and more focus is being placed on this important process, thus assisting women to be more successful in the future.

This book started with a cartoon on flying pigs and the concept that it is impossible for pigs to fly. This book will end with the concept that pigs can fly if they really want to and believe that flying is possible or even probable. The same is true of working women, we can succeed if we really want to.

There are flying pigs!

Did you borrow this copy?

Order your own copy of *The Book For Working Women.*

This book was written to raise money to fund scholarships for women in Chemistry.

The official price of this book is $17.50 ($15 plus $2.50 for postage and handling). Foreign orders add $2 for shipping. The price includes a $10.00 tax-deductible contribution to the scholarship fund of Promethium Chapter of Iota Sigma Pi.

Originally the price was $30 with a $25 contribution to the scholarship fund. We have lowered the contribution to make the book more accessible. Additional contributions to the scholarship fund of Promethium Chapter of Iota Sigma Pi are of course welcomed and appreciated.

Call Aha Publishing at (503) 626-5114 or J. P. Kilbourn, Ph.D. at (503) 222-5279 for quantity discounts.

Name _____

Address _____

City, State, ZIP _____

Number of copies ordered _____

Check enclosed for _____

Send your order to: **Aha Publishing**
13275 S. W. Hazel
Beaverton, OR 97005

                  or

J. P. Kilbourn, Ph.D.
3178 S. W. Fairmount Blvd.
Portland, OR 97201